Operation Overlord: The Spies Who Saved D-Day

Copyright Page

TITLE: Operation Overlord: The Spies who Saved D-Day

1ST Edition

ISBN: 9798223424819

Table of Contents

Operation Overlord: The Spies who Saved D-Day

By Roberto Miguel Rodriguez

Dear Historians and Students of History,

Welcome to "The Spies Who Saved D-Day: Intelligence and Espionage in Operation Overlord." This book delves into the intricate world of intelligence and espionage during one of the most pivotal moments in history, the Allied invasion of Normandy in 1944.

Operation Overlord, the 1944 Allied Invasion of Normandy during World War II, was a monumental military undertaking that required meticulous planning and precise execution. This subchapter aims to highlight the flexibility and adaptability of the book's outline to cater to the needs and preferences of both the author and our esteemed audience.

Here, we explore the various aspects of Operation Overlord that historians find intriguing. From the military strategy and planning during the invasion to the critical role of intelligence and espionage, we delve into the details that made this operation a success. We analyze the naval operations and amphibious warfare that played a crucial role in the Normandy invasion and the airborne operations and paratrooper missions that were instrumental in establishing a foothold in enemy territory.

Furthermore, we examine the role of specific military units or divisions in the Normandy invasion, shedding light on their contributions and sacrifices. Weather conditions played a significant role in Operation Overlord, and we explore their impact on the operation's success or failure. Additionally, we delve into the role of technology and innovation in supporting the Allied invasion, discussing the advancements that aided the troops on the ground.

We also address the medical and logistical challenges faced during Operation Overlord, highlighting the immense efforts required to sustain such a massive operation. Furthermore, we delve into the experiences of civilians and resistance movements in Normandy during the invasion, acknowledging their courage and resilience.

Lastly, we reflect on the long-term consequences and legacy of Operation Overlord, examining its impact on subsequent military campaigns and the world as a whole.

It is important to note that this book outline is a suggestion and can be modified or expanded upon to suit the specific needs and preferences of both the author and our target audience. We encourage you, as historians and experts in this field, to contribute your insights and perspectives, ensuring that this book becomes a comprehensive and authoritative resource on the subject.

Thank you for embarking on this historical journey with us.

Yours sincerely,

The Author

Introduction

The Normandy Landings, also known as D-Day, marked a pivotal turning point in World War II and forever changed the course of history. On June 6, 1944, Allied forces launched a daring amphibious assault on the beaches of Normandy, France, in an operation codenamed Operation Overlord. This subchapter seeks to commemorate the heroes of that fateful day and explore the lasting legacy of the Normandy Landings.

Operation Overlord was meticulously planned, with military strategy and intelligence playing a crucial role in its success. Historians have extensively studied the complex planning and coordination that went into the invasion. The subchapter delves into the military strategy and planning during Operation Overlord, highlighting the meticulous attention to detail and the innovative tactics employed by the Allied forces.

Intelligence and espionage were instrumental in the success of Operation Overlord. The subchapter sheds light on the vital role played by intelligence agencies and spies in gathering crucial information on German defenses, troop movements, and strategic targets. It explores how the intelligence gathered by these unsung heroes helped shape the outcome of the invasion.

Naval operations and amphibious warfare were key components of the Normandy invasion. The subchapter examines the challenges faced by the Allied naval forces and the amphibious tactics employed to overcome them. It also discusses the critical role played by specialized military units and divisions in the invasion.

Airborne operations and paratrooper missions were another crucial aspect of Operation Overlord. The subchapter explores the daring actions of the paratroopers who were dropped behind enemy lines, disrupting German defenses and securing strategic positions.

The impact of weather conditions on Operation Overlord cannot be overstated. The subchapter explores the challenges posed by unpredictable weather and how it affected the timing and execution of the invasion.

Furthermore, the subchapter delves into the role of technology and innovation in supporting the Allied invasion, including the development of specialized landing craft, weapons, and communication systems. It also addresses the medical and logistical challenges faced by the Allied forces during the invasion, as well as the heroic efforts of medical personnel and support units. The subchapter acknowledges the courage and resilience of the Normandy civilians and resistance movements, who provided invaluable support to the Allied forces during the invasion.

Lastly, it examines the long-term consequences and legacy of Operation Overlord. The Normandy Landings not only led to the liberation of France but also played a crucial role in the ultimate defeat of Nazi Germany. The subchapter explores how this historic event continues to shape our understanding of military strategy, intelligence gathering, and the sacrifices made by the heroes of D-Day.

In conclusion, the subchapter "Commemorating the Heroes of D-Day: The Normandy Landings' Legacy" pays tribute to the brave men and women who participated in the Normandy Landings and explores the lasting impact of Operation Overlord on military history and the world at large.

Chapter 1: The Planning and Preparation of Operation Overlord

The Origins and Objectives of Operation Overlord

Operation Overlord, the codename for the Allied invasion of Normandy during World War II, was a meticulously planned military operation that aimed to liberate Western Europe from Nazi occupation. This subchapter delves into the origins and objectives of Operation Overlord, providing a comprehensive understanding of the events that led to this pivotal moment in history.

The seeds of Operation Overlord were sown in the early years of World War II, as the Allied forces sought to formulate a grand strategy to defeat the Axis powers. With the fall of France in 1940 and the subsequent evacuation of British and French forces from Dunkirk, it became clear that a cross-Channel invasion was necessary to turn the tide of the war. The planning for Operation Overlord began in earnest in 1943, with the appointment of General Dwight D. Eisenhower as the Supreme Commander of the Allied Expeditionary Force.

The primary objective of Operation Overlord was to establish a beachhead in Normandy, from where the Allied forces could launch a full-scale invasion of Western Europe. The invasion was intended to catch the Germans off guard, forcing them to divert their attention and resources from the Eastern Front, where they were engaged in a bitter struggle against the Soviet Union. The success of Operation Overlord hinged on a combination of careful planning, intelligence gathering, and technological innovation.

Intelligence and espionage played a crucial role in the success of Operation Overlord. Allied intelligence agencies, such as the British Special Operations Executive (SOE) and the American Office of

Strategic Services (OSS), gathered vital information on German defenses, troop deployments, and fortifications along the Normandy coast. This intelligence was used to identify suitable landing sites, plan amphibious and airborne operations, and devise effective strategies to overcome the formidable German defenses.

Naval operations and amphibious warfare were instrumental in the Normandy invasion. The Allies assembled a vast armada of ships, landing craft, and support vessels to transport troops, equipment, and supplies across the English Channel. The amphibious assault on the Normandy beaches on June 6, 1944, involved a complex and coordinated effort involving naval bombardment, airborne drops, and the storming of fortified positions by ground forces.

Airborne operations and paratrooper missions were a key component of Operation Overlord. Thousands of paratroopers from the American 82nd and 101st Airborne Divisions, as well as the British 6th Airborne Division, were dropped behind enemy lines to secure key objectives and disrupt German defenses. Their bravery and determination played a crucial role in the success of the invasion.

The role of specific military units and divisions cannot be understated in the Normandy invasion. The British and Canadian forces played a significant role in securing the eastern flank of the Normandy beaches, while the American forces spearheaded the assault on the western beaches. The success of the invasion relied on the coordination and cooperation of these diverse military units.

Weather conditions posed significant challenges to Operation Overlord. The invasion was originally scheduled for June 5, 1944, but was delayed by a day due to unfavorable weather conditions. Despite this, the weather on June 6 was far from ideal, with rough seas and low cloud cover. However, the Allied commanders decided to press ahead with the invasion, and their gamble paid off.

Technological innovation played a vital role in supporting the Allied invasion. The development of specialized landing craft, such as the Higgins boat and the Duplex Drive (DD) tank, enabled the troops and equipment to be landed directly onto the beaches. The Allies also made use of advanced radar systems, code-breaking techniques, and deception tactics to gain a strategic advantage over the Germans.

The logistical and medical challenges during Operation Overlord were immense. The successful execution of the invasion required a massive logistical effort, involving the transportation of troops, equipment, and supplies across the English Channel. The medical teams faced the daunting task of treating and evacuating the wounded amidst the chaos of battle.

Civilians and resistance movements in Normandy played a crucial role in supporting the invasion. The French Resistance provided invaluable intelligence and assistance to the Allied forces, sabotaging German infrastructure and disrupting communications. The local population also played a critical role in providing food, shelter, and support to the invading troops.

The long-term consequences and legacy of Operation Overlord are far-reaching. The successful invasion of Normandy marked a turning point in the war, leading to the liberation of Western Europe from Nazi tyranny. It showcased the effectiveness of large-scale coordinated military operations and set the stage for the eventual defeat of Germany. Operation Overlord remains a testament to the bravery, sacrifice, and ingenuity of the Allied forces and continues to be studied by historians as a model of military strategy and planning.

The Strategic Importance of Normandy

In the grand tapestry of World War II, few chapters stand out as prominently as Operation Overlord, the Allied invasion of Normandy.

This audacious military campaign, which unfolded on the beaches of northern France in June 1944, forever altered the course of the war. The strategic importance of Normandy cannot be overstated, as it formed the linchpin of the Allies' plan to liberate Western Europe from the clutches of Nazi Germany.

From a military strategy and planning perspective, Normandy offered several crucial advantages. Its proximity to the British Isles made it an ideal launching point for the invasion, allowing the Allies to amass a formidable force without alerting the Germans. Moreover, the region's geography provided a diverse array of landing options, enabling the Allies to exploit the element of surprise and overwhelm German defenses.

However, the success of Operation Overlord hinged not only on military might but also on intelligence and espionage. In the months leading up to the invasion, an elaborate network of spies and intelligence operatives worked tirelessly to gather vital information about German defenses, troop deployments, and coastal fortifications. These intelligence insights were instrumental in shaping the invasion plans, helping the Allies identify the most vulnerable points along the Normandy coast and devise effective strategies to neutralize them.

Naval operations and amphibious warfare played a pivotal role in the Normandy invasion. The Allies assembled a massive armada of ships and landing craft, which ferried troops, equipment, and supplies across the English Channel. The ability to successfully coordinate these complex naval operations, despite the treacherous waters and German naval threats, was a testament to the meticulous planning and expertise of the Allied forces.

Similarly, airborne operations and paratrooper missions were critical in securing key objectives behind enemy lines. The daring exploits of paratroopers from the 101st and 82nd Airborne Divisions, who dropped deep into enemy territory to disrupt German defenses, played a decisive role in the success of the invasion.

The Normandy invasion also witnessed the participation of specific military units and divisions that left an indelible mark on history. From the valiant efforts of the British 6th Airborne Division in capturing key bridges to the heroism displayed by the American 1st Infantry Division on Omaha Beach, these units demonstrated unparalleled bravery and determination.

Weather conditions posed an unpredictable challenge during Operation Overlord. The invasion was initially scheduled for June 5th, 1944, but had to be postponed by a day due to poor weather. The impact of weather on the success of the invasion cannot be underestimated, as it influenced the timing, logistics, and effectiveness of the Allied assault.

Technology and innovation played a crucial role in supporting the Allied invasion. From the development of specialized landing craft, such as the Higgins boats, to the deployment of innovative weapons and equipment, such as the Mulberry harbors and the "Hobart's Funnies" tanks, the Allies leveraged technological advancements to overcome the formidable obstacles posed by the German defenses.

Operation Overlord's legacy extends far beyond its immediate impact on the war. The invasion marked a turning point in the conflict, signaling the beginning of the end for Nazi Germany. The successful liberation of Western Europe bolstered Allied morale, shattered the myth of German invincibility, and paved the way for the eventual Allied victory.

In conclusion, the strategic importance of Normandy in the context of Operation Overlord cannot be overstated. From military strategy and planning to intelligence and espionage, naval operations to airborne missions, specific military units to weather conditions, technology and innovation to the legacy of the invasion, every aspect of the Normandy campaign played a critical role in the ultimate success of the Allies. The events that unfolded on the beaches of Normandy in 1944 forever shaped the course of history, cementing the importance of this iconic chapter in World War II.

Allied Military Command Structure

In the grand operation that was Operation Overlord, the success of the Allied invasion of Normandy during World War II was heavily reliant on a robust and efficient military command structure. The coordination and collaboration among the various military branches was crucial in ensuring the success of the invasion, and this subchapter aims to delve into the intricacies of the Allied Military Command Structure.

At the helm of the command structure was General Dwight D. Eisenhower, the Supreme Commander of the Allied Expeditionary Force. Under his leadership, the command structure was divided into three major components: ground, air, and naval forces. Each component consisted of several subcommands, divisions, and units, all working in unison to achieve the common objective of liberating Western Europe from Nazi occupation.

The ground forces were under the command of General Bernard Montgomery, who was responsible for planning and executing the amphibious landings on the beaches of Normandy. The air forces, led by Air Chief Marshal Trafford Leigh-Mallory, played a pivotal role in providing air cover, conducting strategic bombing missions, and carrying out airborne operations. The naval forces, under Admiral Bertram Ramsay, were responsible for the complex task of transporting troops, equipment, and supplies across the English Channel and providing fire support during the landings.

The success of the military command structure was greatly influenced by the role of intelligence and espionage. Through meticulous gathering and analysis of intelligence, the Allies were able to gather crucial information about the German defenses, fortifications, and troop movements. This intelligence was essential in determining the timing, location, and scale of the invasion, allowing the Allied forces to exploit weaknesses in the German defenses and achieve surprise.

Furthermore, the command structure also had to contend with the challenges posed by weather conditions, technological limitations, logistical constraints, and medical issues. The unpredictable weather in the English Channel heavily influenced the timing of the invasion, as the success of the amphibious landings was contingent on favorable tides and weather conditions. Technological innovations such as the Mulberry harbors, PLUTO pipeline, and artificial harbors provided vital support to the invasion, facilitating the rapid buildup of troops and supplies on the beaches of Normandy.

The Allied Military Command Structure was not just limited to military personnel but also involved the participation of civilians and resistance movements in Normandy. The French resistance played a crucial role in sabotaging German supply lines and providing valuable intelligence to the Allies, greatly aiding the success of the invasion.

In conclusion, the Allied Military Command Structure was a well-coordinated and multifaceted entity that played a pivotal role in the success of Operation Overlord. The collaboration among the ground, air, and naval forces, supported by intelligence and espionage, technology and innovation, and the involvement of civilians and resistance movements, ensured the triumph of the Allied invasion of Normandy. The legacy of Operation Overlord and the strategic lessons learned from this military endeavor continue to shape military strategy and planning to this day.

The Selection of General Dwight D. Eisenhower as Supreme Commander

In the annals of military history, few decisions have had a more profound impact on the outcome of a war than the selection of General Dwight D. Eisenhower as the Supreme Commander of the Allied forces for Operation Overlord. As historians of World War II are well aware, the success of this ambitious invasion hinged not only on meticulous planning and strategy but also on the leadership and charisma of the man at the helm.

Eisenhower's appointment as Supreme Commander was far from arbitrary. His exceptional leadership qualities and experience made him the ideal candidate for such a monumental task. Having previously served as the Supreme Allied Commander in the Mediterranean Theater, Eisenhower had gained invaluable experience in coordinating complex multinational operations.

One of Eisenhower's most notable strengths was his skill in building and maintaining strong relationships with key figures in the Allied forces. His diplomatic prowess was crucial in ensuring the cooperation and unity necessary for the success of Operation Overlord. Eisenhower's ability to work effectively with leaders such as Winston Churchill and General Bernard Montgomery played a pivotal role in the planning and execution of the invasion.

Furthermore, Eisenhower's strategic acumen was instrumental in shaping the overall military plan for Operation Overlord. Understanding the importance of surprise and deception, he oversaw the development and execution of Operation Bodyguard, a comprehensive deception plan aimed at misleading the German High Command regarding the location and timing of the invasion. This intricate web of misinformation played a crucial role in the eventual success of the Normandy invasion.

Eisenhower's selection also underscored the importance of intelligence and espionage in the success of Operation Overlord. Recognizing the need for accurate and timely information, Eisenhower established a robust intelligence network that relied on the expertise of skilled intelligence officers and the invaluable contributions of resistance movements in occupied Europe. This intelligence network provided critical insights into German defenses, enabling Eisenhower to make informed decisions regarding the timing and location of the invasion.

In conclusion, the selection of General Dwight D. Eisenhower as Supreme Commander for Operation Overlord was a masterstroke that set the stage for one of the most significant military operations in history. Eisenhower's leadership, strategic vision, and ability to forge strong alliances were instrumental in the success of the invasion. Moreover, his recognition of the critical role played by intelligence and espionage ensured that the Allied forces were well-informed and prepared for the challenges ahead. The legacy of Eisenhower's leadership in Operation Overlord continues to resonate, not only in military strategy and planning but also in the enduring lessons it provides for future generations.

Chapter 2: Military Strategy and Planning during Operation Overlord

The Debate over the Invasion Strategy

In the heart of World War II, the stage was set for one of the most audacious operations in military history - Operation Overlord, the Allied invasion of Normandy. However, before the troops could storm the beaches of France, there was a heated debate among military strategists regarding the best approach to execute this daring mission.

The invasion strategy debate revolved around several key issues that would ultimately shape the success of Operation Overlord. One of the main points of contention was whether to launch a direct assault on the heavily fortified German defenses or to employ a diversionary tactic to confuse the enemy.

Some argued that a direct assault, with a concentrated force hitting the beaches head-on, would be the most effective way to quickly establish a beachhead and push inland. Others, however, believed that a diversionary tactic, such as a feigned attack at Calais, would draw German forces away from Normandy, allowing the Allied troops to gain a foothold with less resistance.

Another aspect of the strategy that was hotly debated was the role of intelligence and espionage in the success of the invasion. Some believed that relying heavily on intelligence reports and covert operations could provide the necessary information to exploit weaknesses in the German defenses. Others were skeptical about the reliability of intelligence and argued for a more cautious approach, relying primarily on the strength of the Allied forces.

Furthermore, the debate also encompassed the role of specific military units or divisions in the Normandy invasion. Some argued for the use of airborne operations and paratrooper missions to secure key objectives and disrupt enemy defenses before the amphibious landings. Others were skeptical about the effectiveness of these operations and advocated for a more traditional approach.

The impact of weather conditions on Operation Overlord was another contentious issue. The invasion had to be timed perfectly to take advantage of the tides and moonlight, while also considering the unpredictable nature of the English Channel. Some argued for a delay in the invasion due to unfavorable weather conditions, while others believed that the element of surprise was of paramount importance, regardless of the weather.

Ultimately, the debate over the invasion strategy was a reflection of the complexity and enormity of Operation Overlord. It highlighted the different perspectives and expertise of the military strategists involved. The decisions made in this debate would have far-reaching consequences not only for the success of the invasion but also for the future of the war and the legacy of Operation Overlord.

The Development of the Overlord Plan

The success of Operation Overlord, the Allied invasion of Normandy during World War II, was the result of meticulous planning and strategic thinking. The development of the Overlord plan was a complex and multifaceted process that involved the collaboration of military strategists, intelligence officers, and espionage agents. This subchapter delves into the detailed account of the planning and development of the Overlord plan, shedding light on the crucial role played by intelligence and espionage in its success.

The Overlord plan was devised in response to the need for a large-scale invasion of Nazi-occupied Europe. The invasion, codenamed Operation Overlord, aimed to establish a Western front and liberate France from German control. The planning process began with an analysis of previous amphibious operations, such as the Dieppe Raid in 1942, which provided valuable insights into the challenges and pitfalls of such large-scale assaults.

Military strategists, led by General Dwight D. Eisenhower, meticulously studied the geography, tides, and weather patterns of the Normandy coastline. They realized that the success of the invasion hinged on surprise and speed, as well as the ability to secure a beachhead quickly. To achieve this, the plan incorporated innovative tactics such as the use of artificial harbors, known as Mulberries, to support the logistical needs of the invading forces.

Intelligence played a pivotal role in shaping the Overlord plan. Intelligence officers and espionage agents gathered crucial information about German defenses, troop movements, and the mindset of the enemy. This information was used to identify the most vulnerable points along the Normandy coastline and to devise strategies to exploit these weaknesses.

The plan also relied heavily on naval and airborne operations. Extensive preparations were made to transport and deploy troops, vehicles, and supplies by sea and air. Naval forces played a vital role in securing the sea lanes and providing fire support for the ground troops. Airborne units, including paratroopers, were tasked with disrupting German defenses and securing key objectives in the early stages of the invasion.

The development of the Overlord plan was not without challenges. The unpredictable weather conditions in the English Channel posed a significant threat to the success of the operation. The invasion had to be carefully timed to coincide with favorable tides and weather conditions.

The plan also had to account for the logistical challenges of supplying and sustaining a large invading force on enemy territory.

The success of the Overlord plan ultimately hinged on the courage and determination of the soldiers who landed on the beaches of Normandy on June 6, 1944. Their sacrifices, combined with the meticulous planning, strategic thinking, and the invaluable contributions of intelligence and espionage, paved the way for the liberation of France and the eventual defeat of Nazi Germany. The legacy of Operation Overlord remains a testament to the power of meticulous planning, intelligence gathering, and the indomitable spirit of those who fought for freedom.

Securing Air Superiority over Normandy

During the planning stages of Operation Overlord, the Allied commanders recognized the crucial importance of securing air superiority over Normandy. This subchapter delves into the intricate strategies, intelligence, and espionage efforts that played a significant role in achieving this objective.

The success of Operation Overlord hinged on the ability of the Allied forces to establish air dominance over the invasion area. Without control of the skies, the amphibious assault and subsequent ground operations would have been rendered extremely vulnerable to enemy air attacks. Thus, meticulous planning and coordination were required to neutralize the German Luftwaffe.

The intelligence gathered by the Allies proved invaluable in their efforts to secure air superiority. Through espionage networks and code-breaking operations, they were able to obtain critical information on enemy air defenses, radar systems, and the disposition of Luftwaffe forces. This intelligence allowed the Allies to develop effective countermeasures and devise strategies to exploit gaps in the German air defenses.

One of the key aspects of securing air superiority was the strategic bombing campaign carried out by the Allied air forces. With intelligence guiding their targets, the bombers relentlessly targeted German airfields, communication lines, and radar installations. This not only weakened the Luftwaffe's ability to respond effectively but also disrupted their command and control infrastructure.

Naval operations also played a crucial role in securing air superiority. The Allied navies worked tirelessly to establish a protective umbrella off the coast of Normandy, preventing German aircraft from reaching the invasion area. This allowed the Allied aircraft to operate with relative impunity, conducting reconnaissance missions, suppressing enemy defenses, and providing close air support to the ground forces.

Furthermore, airborne operations and paratrooper missions were instrumental in securing key objectives behind enemy lines. Paratroopers were dropped in the early hours of D-Day to disrupt German communications, destroy infrastructure, and seize vital bridges and crossroads. By doing so, they prevented the Germans from effectively reinforcing their defenses and hindered their ability to launch counterattacks.

The success of securing air superiority was not without challenges. The German Luftwaffe put up fierce resistance, and the Allies had to confront advanced aircraft, skilled pilots, and relentless air defense systems. Additionally, adverse weather conditions, such as fog and low cloud cover, posed significant challenges to the Allied air forces.

Securing air superiority over Normandy was a critical element of Operation Overlord's success. The combination of intelligence gathering, strategic bombing, naval operations, and airborne missions proved pivotal in neutralizing the Luftwaffe and allowing the invasion to proceed unhindered. By controlling the skies, the Allies gained a significant advantage, paving the way for the success of the largest amphibious assault in history.

This subchapter provides a comprehensive analysis of the planning, execution, and impact of securing air superiority over Normandy, shedding light on the crucial role played by intelligence, strategic bombing, naval operations, and airborne missions. It serves as a valuable resource for historians seeking to understand the complexities and significance of this pivotal aspect of Operation Overlord.

The Role of Deception in Operation Bodyguard

Deception played a vital role in the success of Operation Bodyguard, a crucial component of the larger Operation Overlord. As historians delve into the intricate details of this remarkable intelligence and espionage operation, it becomes evident that the Allies' ability to deceive the Germans was instrumental in the Allied invasion of Normandy during World War II.

Operation Bodyguard was a complex web of deception, designed specifically to mislead the German High Command about the timing, location, and scale of the Allied invasion. It comprised several sub-plans, each with its own unique objective and supported by a range of innovative strategies.

The overarching goal of Operation Bodyguard was to convince the Germans that the main Allied invasion would occur at the Pas de Calais, rather than the actual target of Normandy. Through a combination of double agents, false radio transmissions, and fictional military units, the Allies created an elaborate illusion that successfully diverted German attention away from the Normandy coast.

One of the key elements of Operation Bodyguard was the creation of a fictional army, known as the First United States Army Group (FUSAG). This imaginary force, under the command of General George S. Patton, was stationed near Dover and actively promoted as the main strike force against the Germans. The Allies used inflatable tanks, dummy landing craft, and even phony radio traffic to give the illusion of a massive buildup of troops in the region.

Furthermore, the Allies employed a network of double agents, such as the infamous Juan Pujol Garcia (codenamed Garbo), to feed the Germans false information. Garbo, a Spanish national working on behalf of the Allies, convinced the Germans that he had a network of informants across Britain, providing them with highly credible but entirely fictional intelligence.

The success of Operation Bodyguard can be attributed to the meticulous planning and execution of these deception efforts. By keeping the Germans guessing and diverting their attention away from Normandy, the Allies gained a significant advantage. The Germans, convinced that the main attack would come at Pas de Calais, kept their best troops and resources deployed far from the actual landing sites at Normandy, greatly facilitating the success of the invasion.

The role of deception in Operation Bodyguard underscores the critical importance of intelligence and espionage in the success of Operation Overlord. By effectively utilizing deceptive tactics, the Allies were able to outmaneuver the Germans and secure a foothold in Normandy, ultimately leading to the liberation of Europe from Nazi occupation.

For historians studying Operation Overlord, understanding the intricate details of the deception employed in Operation Bodyguard provides valuable insights into the military strategy and planning that contributed to the success of the Allied invasion. It also highlights the significant role of specific military units and the impact of weather conditions on the operation. Furthermore, the long-term consequences and legacy of Operation Overlord can be better appreciated through an examination of the intelligence and espionage efforts that played a vital role in its success.

In conclusion, Operation Bodyguard's use of deception was a pivotal factor in the success of Operation Overlord. This subchapter sheds light on the significant role of deception in military strategy and planning, the impact of intelligence and espionage, and the long-lasting consequences and legacy of the Allied invasion of Normandy. Historians exploring Operation Overlord and its various niches will find this exploration of deception in Operation Bodyguard to be a fascinating and crucial aspect of their research.

Chapter 3: Intelligence and Espionage in the Success of Operation Overlord

The Work of the Allied Intelligence Agencies

The success of Operation Overlord, the 1944 Allied invasion of Normandy during World War II, can be attributed in large part to the crucial work of the intelligence agencies involved. These agencies, which included the British Secret Intelligence Service (MI6), the United States Office of Strategic Services (OSS), and the French Resistance, played a vital role in gathering information, conducting espionage, and providing strategic guidance to the military planners.

Operating in a highly complex and risky environment, the intelligence agencies faced numerous challenges. One of the key tasks was to gather accurate and up-to-date information about German defenses along the Normandy coast. This required a combination of human intelligence, signals intelligence, and aerial reconnaissance. Intelligence officers risked their lives by infiltrating Nazi-occupied territory, gathering information from local sources, and relaying it back to their headquarters.

The intelligence agencies also played a critical role in planning and coordinating the amphibious and airborne operations during Operation Overlord. They identified potential landing sites, assessed the strength of German defenses, and provided recommendations on the timing and sequencing of the assaults. This information was crucial in ensuring the success of the initial D-Day landings.

Furthermore, the intelligence agencies were instrumental in supporting specific military units and divisions during the Normandy invasion. They provided them with detailed maps, target lists, and information on enemy troop movements. This enabled the Allied forces to exploit weaknesses in the German defenses and achieve tactical superiority.

The impact of weather conditions on Operation Overlord cannot be overstated, and the intelligence agencies were well aware of this. They closely monitored weather patterns and provided regular updates to the military planners. This allowed them to choose the most favorable conditions for the invasion, which eventually took place on June 6, 1944.

The role of technology and innovation in supporting the Allied invasion cannot be overlooked either. The intelligence agencies were at the forefront of developing new technologies, such as radar and code-breaking machines, which proved instrumental in gathering intelligence and decrypting German communications. These technological advancements gave the Allies a significant advantage in understanding the enemy's intentions and capabilities.

In addition to their military contributions, the intelligence agencies also worked closely with the French Resistance and civilians in Normandy. They provided them with training, equipment, and support, enabling them to carry out acts of sabotage, gather intelligence, and disrupt German operations. The resistance movements played a crucial role in weakening the German defenses and creating chaos behind enemy lines.

The legacy of the intelligence agencies' work in Operation Overlord is undeniable. Their contributions not only ensured the success of the invasion but also paved the way for subsequent Allied victories in Europe. The lessons learned from their efforts continue to shape military strategy and planning to this day, highlighting the enduring importance of intelligence and espionage in warfare.

Gathering and Analyzing Intelligence

In the grand tapestry of Operation Overlord, one cannot underestimate the critical role played by intelligence and espionage. As historians, it is our duty to delve into the depths of this chapter, exploring the intricacies of gathering and analyzing intelligence that ultimately proved instrumental in the success of the Allied invasion of Normandy during World War II.

Military strategy and planning during Operation Overlord relied heavily on the intelligence gathered by various intelligence agencies and operatives. The painstaking work of spies allowed the Allies to gain a crucial understanding of enemy positions, fortifications, and troop movements. The information obtained from these sources shaped the overall plan, enabling the Allied forces to exploit weaknesses and launch targeted attacks that ultimately led to victory.

Naval operations and amphibious warfare in the Normandy invasion were also heavily influenced by intelligence. The knowledge of German coastal defenses, including mines, obstacles, and gun emplacements, allowed the Allies to plan their amphibious landings with precision. By analyzing intelligence reports on tidal patterns and weather conditions, they strategically chose the optimal time for the invasion, mitigating risks and maximizing their chances of success.

Similarly, airborne operations and paratrooper missions during Operation Overlord were meticulously planned using intelligence. By identifying drop zones and assessing enemy resistance, the Allies were able to deploy paratroopers behind enemy lines, disrupting German communications and securing vital objectives. The invaluable intelligence gathered by these operatives significantly contributed to the overall success of the invasion.

Specific military units and divisions played crucial roles in the Normandy invasion, and much of their success can be attributed to the intelligence they received. By understanding German tactics, troop movements, and supply lines, these units were able to adapt their strategies and make informed decisions on the battlefield.

The impact of weather conditions on Operation Overlord cannot be overstated. Intelligence reports on the weather played a significant role in deciding the date of the invasion. The success of the entire operation hinged on the ability of the Allied forces to secure a foothold on the beaches, and any adverse weather conditions could have spelled disaster.

Technology and innovation also played a vital role in supporting the Allied invasion. From radar systems that detected German aircraft to the development of new weapons and vehicles, intelligence on enemy technology allowed the Allies to gain a technological edge.

As historians, it is essential to recognize the challenges faced by medical and logistical teams during Operation Overlord. The intelligence gathered on medical facilities, supply routes, and logistical challenges helped ensure that the necessary resources were in place to support the invasion and treat the wounded.

The involvement of civilians and resistance movements in Normandy during the invasion was another critical aspect shaped by intelligence. By working closely with resistance fighters, intelligence agencies were able to gather critical information on German activities, sabotage enemy defenses, and provide valuable assistance to the Allied forces.

Finally, the long-term consequences and legacy of Operation Overlord owe a great deal to the intelligence and espionage efforts during the invasion. The success of the operation not only turned the tide of the war but also paved the way for future intelligence operations and shaped military strategies for years to come.

In conclusion, gathering and analyzing intelligence proved to be indispensable in the success of Operation Overlord. The meticulous work of spies, the analysis of information, and the utilization of technology all played a pivotal role. By understanding the significance of intelligence in this historic event, historians can gain a deeper appreciation for the intricate web of factors that culminated in the triumph of the Allied forces in Normandy.

The Use of Double Agents and Codebreaking

In the annals of military history, few operations have been as pivotal and complex as Operation Overlord, the Allied invasion of Normandy during World War II. The success of this daring endeavor hinged not only on meticulous planning, brave soldiers, and superior tactics but also on the crucial role played by intelligence and espionage. Within this dynamic landscape, the use of double agents and codebreaking emerged as vital components that significantly contributed to the triumph of Operation Overlord.

Double agents, individuals who surreptitiously work for opposing sides, played a crucial role in deceiving the enemy and gathering critical information. These intrepid individuals infiltrated enemy ranks, meticulously feeding misinformation and creating confusion among German forces. Their invaluable contributions helped to divert German attention away from the actual invasion site, enabling the Allies to land relatively unopposed on the Normandy beaches. Historians have since hailed the exploits of double agents such as Juan Pujol Garcia (codenamed "Garbo") and Dušan Popov (codenamed "Tricycle"), whose audacious acts of deception helped shape the outcome of Operation Overlord.

Simultaneously, codebreaking emerged as a game-changer in the intelligence war. The British Government Code and Cypher School at Bletchley Park, led by the brilliant mathematician Alan Turing, tirelessly worked to decipher the formidable Enigma machine codes used by the Germans. Breaking these codes provided the Allies with invaluable insights into German military plans, troop movements, and strategic intentions. The decoded information allowed military strategists to anticipate German counterattacks and adjust their own plans accordingly, thus ensuring the success of the invasion. The role of codebreaking in Operation Overlord demonstrated the power of intelligence and innovation in shaping the outcome of large-scale military operations.

The use of double agents and codebreaking during Operation Overlord left an indelible mark on military strategy and planning. Their successful deployment paved the way for future operations, where intelligence and espionage played an increasingly significant role. The lessons learned from their use in Normandy influenced subsequent military campaigns, showcasing the critical importance of gathering accurate and timely information to achieve victory.

As historians delve into the intricacies of Operation Overlord, it becomes evident that the use of double agents and codebreaking were instrumental in the success of the invasion. The bravery and ingenuity of these individuals, coupled with the innovative techniques employed, not only saved countless lives but also secured a crucial turning point in World War II. The legacy of their contributions reverberates to this day, reminding us of the enduring power of intelligence and espionage in shaping the course of history.

The Importance of Ultra Intelligence

In the annals of military history, few operations have been as meticulously planned and executed as Operation Overlord, the Allied invasion of Normandy during World War II. The success of this audacious undertaking was not solely dependent on the bravery and skill of the soldiers storming the beaches; it was equally reliant on a less visible yet equally crucial factor: ultra intelligence.

Ultra intelligence, derived from the decryption of German Enigma machine codes, provided Allied commanders with invaluable information regarding enemy positions, strategies, and intentions. This intelligence gave the Allies a critical advantage, allowing them to plan their operations with precision and exploit the weaknesses of the German defenses.

One of the most significant contributions of ultra intelligence was in the area of military strategy and planning during Operation Overlord. By intercepting and deciphering German communications, the Allies were able to gain a comprehensive understanding of the enemy's defensive preparations along the Normandy coast. This information enabled them to select the most favorable landing sites and devise effective tactics to overcome the formidable German defenses.

Naval operations and amphibious warfare were central to the success of the Normandy invasion, and ultra intelligence played a pivotal role in these areas as well. Detailed knowledge of German naval movements and minefields allowed the Allies to plan their naval operations with precision, ensuring the safe passage of troops and supplies to the beaches. Additionally, intelligence on German coastal defenses helped the Allies develop effective strategies for neutralizing these obstacles.

Airborne operations and paratrooper missions were another key component of Operation Overlord. Ultra intelligence provided critical information on the deployment and movements of German airborne units, allowing the Allies to plan their own airborne operations accordingly. This intelligence also enabled the Allies to coordinate their efforts with the French Resistance, ensuring that paratroopers were dropped in areas where they would receive maximum support from local resistance fighters.

The role of specific military units and divisions in the Normandy invasion was also influenced by ultra intelligence. The decrypted German communications allowed Allied commanders to identify and target high-value German units, such as armored divisions and elite infantry formations. This information was crucial in determining the allocation of resources and formulating effective strategies to neutralize these threats.

The impact of weather conditions on Operation Overlord cannot be overstated, and once again, ultra intelligence proved instrumental in this regard. By intercepting German weather reports and deciphering their encoded messages, the Allies gained advance knowledge of weather patterns, allowing them to select the most opportune day for the invasion. This intelligence significantly reduced the risks associated with unfavorable weather conditions, ensuring the success of the Allied landings.

In conclusion, the importance of ultra intelligence in the success of Operation Overlord cannot be overstated. It provided the Allies with a decisive advantage by offering unparalleled insights into German military plans, positions, and intentions. Without this critical intelligence, the Normandy invasion would have been a far riskier and less successful endeavor. As historians, it is imperative that we recognize and appreciate the vital role played by ultra intelligence in shaping the course of history.

Chapter 4: Naval Operations and Amphibious Warfare in the Normandy Invasion

The Planning and Execution of the Naval Component

In the grand scope of Operation Overlord, the planning and execution of the naval component stood as a critical pillar in the success of the Allied invasion of Normandy. As historians delve into the intricacies of this monumental military operation, they must acknowledge the immense importance of the naval operations and the strategic brilliance that underpinned its planning and execution.

The Allied forces recognized early on that a successful invasion of Normandy hinged upon securing control of the English Channel. This led to the creation of an expansive naval force, which consisted of a remarkable array of vessels, from battleships and cruisers to landing craft and destroyers. The naval forces were tasked with transporting the troops, their equipment, and supplies across the treacherous waters and onto the beaches of Normandy.

The planning of the naval component was a meticulous endeavor, taking into account various factors such as the tide, weather conditions, and the sheer logistics of moving such a vast number of troops. The naval commanders worked closely with meteorologists to determine the optimal time and date for the invasion, considering the tides and weather patterns that would provide the greatest advantage.

On June 6, 1944, the naval forces launched their assault on the Normandy coast, providing a crucial diversionary tactic to draw German attention away from the airborne and land forces. The naval bombardment that preceded the landing played a vital role in neutralizing enemy defenses and clearing the way for the troops.

The execution of the naval component was a feat of coordination and bravery. Naval officers skillfully maneuvered their vessels through minefields and obstacles, while naval aviators provided air support and reconnaissance. Landing craft ferried troops to the beaches, with naval personnel assisting in the disembarkation process under heavy enemy fire.

The success of the naval operations during the Normandy invasion can be attributed to the careful planning, the courage of the naval personnel, and the invaluable intelligence gathered through espionage. The critical role played by the naval component paved the way for the subsequent success of the airborne and land forces.

In examining the planning and execution of the naval component, historians gain valuable insights into the military strategy and planning during Operation Overlord. They understand the vital role of intelligence and espionage in the success of the operation and how it impacted the overall outcome. Moreover, they recognize the significance of naval operations and amphibious warfare in the Normandy invasion, as well as the role of specific military units and divisions.

The planning and execution of the naval component also shed light on the impact of weather conditions on Operation Overlord and the role of technology and innovation in supporting the Allied invasion. Additionally, historians can explore the medical and logistical challenges faced during the operation, the resilience of civilians and resistance movements in Normandy, and the long-term consequences and legacy of Operation Overlord.

In essence, the planning and execution of the naval component in Operation Overlord exemplify the remarkable coordination, courage, and strategic brilliance that lay at the heart of this pivotal moment in history. By delving into this subchapter, historians gain a comprehensive understanding of the multifaceted aspects of the Normandy invasion and its enduring legacy.

The Role of the Allied Naval Forces

In the grand scheme of Operation Overlord, the successful Allied invasion of Normandy during World War II, the role of the naval forces cannot be overstated. The planning and execution of this amphibious assault required meticulous coordination between the various military branches, and the naval forces played a crucial role in ensuring the success of the mission.

The naval forces were responsible for transporting the troops and supplies across the English Channel, a task that required careful planning and execution. They were also tasked with providing fire support to the troops on the ground, bombarding enemy positions and providing cover for the advancing forces. This was no small feat, as the German defenses were formidable and the success of the invasion hinged on the ability of the naval forces to neutralize them.

The naval forces also played a key role in the airborne operations and paratrooper missions that were carried out as part of Operation Overlord. They provided the necessary transport and support for the paratroopers, dropping them behind enemy lines to disrupt German defenses and secure key objectives. Without the naval forces, these crucial missions would not have been possible.

Furthermore, the naval forces had to contend with the unpredictable and treacherous weather conditions that plagued the Normandy coast. The success of the invasion was heavily dependent on favorable weather, and the naval forces had to adapt and adjust their plans accordingly. They faced strong winds, rough seas, and limited visibility, but they persevered and managed to overcome these challenges.

Technology and innovation also played a significant role in supporting the Allied invasion, and the naval forces were at the forefront of these advancements. They utilized cutting-edge technology such as radar and sonar to detect and track enemy submarines and mines, ensuring the safety of the invasion fleet. They also made use of specialized landing craft and amphibious vehicles, allowing them to transport troops and equipment directly onto the shores of Normandy.

In conclusion, the role of the Allied naval forces in Operation Overlord cannot be understated. They played a crucial role in transporting troops and supplies, providing fire support, conducting airborne operations, and overcoming the challenges posed by the weather and German defenses. Their contributions were instrumental in the success of the invasion and the ultimate liberation of Europe from Nazi occupation.

Overcoming the Challenges of Naval Operations

Naval operations were critical in the success of Operation Overlord, the Allied invasion of Normandy during World War II. The amphibious warfare tactics employed by the Allies were unprecedented and presented numerous challenges that had to be overcome for the invasion to be successful.

One of the primary challenges faced by naval forces was the need to transport and land a massive number of troops and equipment on the beaches of Normandy. This required meticulous planning and coordination, as well as the development of specialized landing craft capable of navigating the treacherous waters and landing troops directly onto the beaches. The naval forces also had to contend with the German coastal defenses, including mines, obstacles, and artillery, which posed a significant threat to the success of the invasion.

Another challenge was the need to maintain control of the seas and protect the invasion fleet from German naval forces. The German navy, although weakened, still posed a threat to the Allied forces. The naval commanders had to deploy their ships strategically to provide protection and support to the landing forces while also engaging the German navy in battle.

The weather conditions also presented a significant challenge. The invasion had to be conducted during a narrow window of opportunity, dictated by the tides and the lunar cycle. The naval commanders had to carefully plan the timing of the invasion to take advantage of the optimal conditions for landing and ensure the success of the operation. However, the weather was unpredictable, and a storm could have resulted in disastrous consequences for the invasion.

Furthermore, the naval forces had to overcome logistical challenges in supplying and supporting the invasion forces. This included transporting troops, equipment, and supplies across the English Channel, establishing and maintaining supply lines, and coordinating with other branches of the military to ensure a steady flow of resources.

Despite these challenges, the naval forces played a crucial role in the success of Operation Overlord. Through meticulous planning, innovative tactics, and the bravery of the sailors, the invasion fleet managed to land thousands of troops on the beaches of Normandy, establishing a foothold that would eventually lead to the liberation of Europe from Nazi occupation.

The legacy of the naval operations during Operation Overlord cannot be overstated. It demonstrated the effectiveness of amphibious warfare and paved the way for future military strategies. The lessons learned from the challenges faced by the naval forces in Normandy continue to inform military planning and operations to this day, making the success of Operation Overlord a testament to the ingenuity, bravery, and determination of those involved.

The Successes and Failures of the Naval Operations

In the massive and complex military operation that was Operation Overlord, the naval operations played a crucial role in the success of the Allied invasion of Normandy during World War II. The amphibious assault on the heavily fortified beaches of Normandy was a daunting task, and the success of this mission hinged on the effectiveness of the naval operations.

The successes of the naval operations were manifold. The planning and coordination between the Allied navies were remarkable, with each fleet assigned specific roles and tasks. The naval forces successfully transported and landed over 156,000 troops on the beaches of Normandy, along with their equipment and supplies. The naval bombardment preceding the landings destroyed key German defenses and allowed the infantry to gain a foothold on the beaches. Additionally, the naval forces provided crucial fire support during the initial assault, suppressing German counterattacks and providing cover for the troops.

However, the naval operations also faced significant challenges and failures. One of the most notable failures was the difficulty in accurately landing troops and equipment on the designated beaches. The strong currents and rough seas caused many landing craft to miss their intended landing zones, leading to confusion and disorganization among the troops. This resulted in the loss of valuable time and the inability to secure key objectives according to the original plan.

Furthermore, the naval operations were also hindered by the German defenses. The German navy and air force launched counterattacks against the Allied naval forces, resulting in the loss of several ships and landing craft. The naval forces had to constantly adapt and improvise to overcome these challenges, which sometimes led to delays and setbacks in the overall operation.

Despite these failures, the naval operations ultimately proved successful in achieving their objectives. The naval forces played a crucial role in establishing a secure beachhead, which allowed for the subsequent deployment of troops, supplies, and equipment. The naval operations also facilitated the evacuation of wounded soldiers and the transport of reinforcements to sustain the momentum of the invasion.

The successes and failures of the naval operations during Operation Overlord serve as a testament to the complexity and difficulties of amphibious warfare. The lessons learned from this operation have informed subsequent military strategies and planning. The role of intelligence and espionage was vital in gathering information about the German defenses and formulating effective naval strategies. The legacy of Operation Overlord continues to shape military operations, highlighting the importance of naval operations in achieving strategic objectives in amphibious assaults.

Chapter 5: Airborne Operations and Paratrooper Missions during Operation Overlord

The Decision to Conduct Airborne Operations

In the planning stages of Operation Overlord, the Allied high command faced a critical decision: whether or not to include airborne operations as part of the invasion strategy. This subchapter aims to explore the factors that influenced this decision and the subsequent impact of airborne operations during the Normandy invasion.

Military strategy and planning during Operation Overlord played a crucial role in the success of the Allied invasion. One key consideration was the need to secure strategic objectives ahead of the amphibious assault. Airborne operations offered a unique opportunity to seize key bridges, disrupt enemy communication lines, and secure vital positions behind enemy lines. Historians studying Operation Overlord must delve into the decision-making process behind the inclusion of airborne operations and its impact on the overall strategy.

Intelligence and espionage were integral to the success of Operation Overlord. The subchapter will highlight the role of intelligence in identifying suitable drop zones and assessing enemy defenses, which informed the decision to conduct airborne operations. The contribution of intelligence operatives in gathering information on German defenses and troop movements will be explored, underscoring the vital role they played in shaping the decision-making process.

Naval operations and amphibious warfare were the primary focus of the Normandy invasion, but airborne operations brought a unique dimension to the operation. By examining the role of specific military units or divisions involved in airborne operations, historians can better understand their impact on the success of the invasion. The subchapter will analyze the achievements and challenges faced by airborne units, such as the 101st and 82nd Airborne Divisions, shedding light on their contributions to the wider campaign.

Weather conditions posed a significant challenge to Operation Overlord, influencing crucial decisions made by Allied commanders. The subchapter will explore how weather conditions impacted the decision to conduct airborne operations and the subsequent outcomes on the ground. This analysis will provide historians with a deeper understanding of the complexities faced by the Allied forces during the invasion.

Lastly, the subchapter will touch upon the long-term consequences and legacy of airborne operations during Operation Overlord. By examining the impact of technology and innovation in supporting the Allied invasion, historians can evaluate the effectiveness of airborne operations and their lasting influence on military strategy. Additionally, the subchapter will discuss the medical and logistical challenges faced by airborne units, as well as the role of civilians and resistance movements in Normandy during the invasion.

In conclusion, the decision to conduct airborne operations during Operation Overlord was a pivotal moment in the planning and execution of the Normandy invasion. By exploring the factors that influenced this decision and examining the subsequent impact on the wider campaign, historians can gain valuable insights into the role of airborne operations in the success of Operation Overlord.

The Training and Preparation of Paratroopers

In the lead-up to Operation Overlord, the Allied invasion of Normandy during World War II, the training and preparation of paratroopers played a pivotal role in the success of the mission. These elite soldiers were tasked with conducting airborne operations, infiltrating enemy territory, and securing key objectives behind enemy lines. This subchapter explores the rigorous training and meticulous preparation that paratroopers underwent in order to carry out their crucial missions.

The training of paratroopers began long before they donned their parachutes. Extensive physical conditioning was paramount, as these soldiers needed to be in peak physical condition to endure the demands of combat. Intense physical training, including endurance runs, obstacle courses, and rigorous strength training, was coupled with combat skills such as marksmanship, hand-to-hand combat, and small unit tactics. Paratroopers were expected to be versatile and adaptable, capable of operating in various environments and under challenging circumstances.

Additionally, paratroopers underwent specialized training in airborne operations. This training encompassed parachute jumps, both static line and freefall, to ensure soldiers were proficient in landing safely and accurately. They also learned how to operate and maintain their equipment, including weapons, radios, and other essential gear. The training emphasized teamwork and cohesion, as paratroopers needed to rely on each other in the chaos of combat.

Preparation for their specific missions was another crucial aspect of paratrooper training. Intelligence and espionage played a significant role in providing paratroopers with vital information about enemy positions, fortifications, and potential threats. This intelligence was used to plan and simulate mission scenarios, allowing paratroopers to familiarize themselves with the objectives and develop strategies for success. Mock missions and live-fire exercises provided practical experience, helping paratroopers refine their skills and build confidence.

The training and preparation of paratroopers were not without challenges. Weather conditions often posed a significant obstacle, as adverse weather could delay or even cancel airborne operations. Paratroopers needed to be adaptable, ready to adjust their plans at a moment's notice. Additionally, medical and logistical challenges were ever-present, as the nature of their missions often meant limited access to medical care and resources. Paratroopers had to rely on their training, resourcefulness, and the support of their fellow soldiers to overcome these obstacles.

The training and preparation of paratroopers were instrumental in the success of Operation Overlord. Their ability to execute their missions with precision and effectiveness allowed the Allied forces to gain a strategic advantage over the enemy. The legacy of these brave soldiers endures, as their contributions in Normandy and beyond have forever shaped the course of history.

Overall, this subchapter highlights the importance of the training and preparation of paratroopers in Operation Overlord. It provides historians with valuable insights into the military strategy, planning, and execution of airborne operations during one of the most significant events of World War II.

The Role of the Airborne Divisions

The success of Operation Overlord, the 1944 Allied Invasion of Normandy during World War II, hinged on a meticulous plan that relied heavily on the role of the airborne divisions. These divisions played a crucial role in setting the stage for the amphibious assault on the Normandy beaches, and their efforts significantly contributed to the overall success of the operation.

The airborne divisions, consisting of paratroopers and glider-borne soldiers, were tasked with securing key objectives behind enemy lines in the early hours of June 6, 1944, commonly known as D-Day. Their primary objectives were to secure and hold bridges, disrupt enemy communications and supply lines, and protect the flanks of the invasion force. By doing so, they aimed to isolate the Normandy beaches and prevent German reinforcements from reaching the invasion area.

The airborne divisions faced numerous challenges during their mission. They had to contend with difficult weather conditions, navigational difficulties, and the risk of being dropped far from their intended drop zones. Despite these challenges, they demonstrated exceptional bravery and adaptability, successfully securing critical objectives and paving the way for the amphibious assault.

One of the most notable successes of the airborne divisions was the capture and defense of key bridges along the Orne and Dives rivers. The British 6th Airborne Division, in particular, accomplished this feat by capturing the strategically important Pegasus Bridge and preventing German counterattacks. This allowed the Allied forces to establish a secure foothold in the area and provided a crucial link between the invasion beaches and the advancing ground forces.

Furthermore, the airborne divisions played a vital role in disrupting enemy communications and supply lines. By sabotaging bridges, destroying roadways, and ambushing German convoys, they effectively hindered the German response to the invasion. Their actions created chaos behind enemy lines, forcing the German forces to divert resources and attention away from the beach defenses.

The success of the airborne divisions during Operation Overlord was the result of meticulous planning, rigorous training, and extraordinary bravery. Their efforts not only secured key objectives but also boosted the morale of the invading forces and instilled a sense of fear and confusion among the German defenders.

The legacy of the airborne divisions' role in Operation Overlord extends far beyond the invasion itself. Their actions paved the way for future airborne operations, revolutionizing military strategy and planning. The lessons learned from their successes and failures continue to shape military doctrine and tactics to this day.

In conclusion, the airborne divisions played a crucial role in the success of Operation Overlord. Their daring actions behind enemy lines secured key objectives, disrupted German communications and supply lines, and paved the way for the amphibious assault. Their efforts not only contributed to the immediate success of the invasion but also had a lasting impact on military strategy and planning. The airborne divisions' bravery and ingenuity in the face of adversity are a testament to the remarkable achievements of the Allied forces during the Normandy invasion.

The Outcomes of the Airborne Operations

The success of Operation Overlord, the 1944 Allied Invasion of Normandy during World War II, hinged on a meticulously planned and executed strategy that involved multiple facets of military operations. One key element that played a crucial role in the success of the invasion was the airborne operations conducted by paratroopers. This subchapter aims to explore the outcomes of these airborne operations and their impact on the overall success of Operation Overlord.

The airborne operations during Operation Overlord were carried out by the British and American forces, with the objective of securing key strategic points behind enemy lines and disrupting German defenses. The main airborne units involved were the British 6th Airborne Division and the American 82nd and 101st Airborne Divisions. These divisions were tasked with capturing and securing vital objectives such as bridges, road junctions, and artillery positions.

The outcomes of the airborne operations were mixed but ultimately contributed significantly to the overall success of Operation Overlord. Despite facing heavy resistance from German forces, the paratroopers managed to achieve several key objectives. For example, the British 6th Airborne Division successfully captured the crucial Pegasus Bridge, which played a vital role in securing the eastern flank of the invasion. The American 82nd and 101st Airborne Divisions also managed to secure important objectives, including the town of Sainte-Mère-Église and key positions around Utah Beach.

By securing these objectives, the paratroopers effectively disrupted German defenses and created chaos in their rear areas. This diversionary tactic drew German forces away from the main invasion beaches, weakening their overall defense and allowing the Allied forces to gain a foothold in Normandy. The airborne operations also helped to establish a link between the invasion forces on the beaches and the paratroopers behind enemy lines, facilitating the consolidation of the invasion and ensuring the success of subsequent operations.

The success of the airborne operations was not without challenges. The paratroopers faced heavy casualties, with many dropping far from their intended drop zones and encountering fierce resistance upon landing. Additionally, the coordination between the paratroopers and the amphibious forces on the beaches was not always smooth, leading to some confusion and delays in achieving their objectives.

Despite these challenges, the outcomes of the airborne operations during Operation Overlord were instrumental in the success of the invasion. By disrupting German defenses and securing key objectives, the paratroopers played a vital role in the overall strategy. Their actions created a significant impact on the German forces, allowing the Allies to establish a strong foothold and ultimately leading to the liberation of occupied Europe.

For historians studying Operation Overlord, understanding the outcomes of the airborne operations provides valuable insights into the military strategy and planning during the invasion. It highlights the importance of intelligence and espionage in identifying key objectives and planning the airborne operations. Furthermore, it sheds light on the role of specific military units or divisions, such as the British 6th Airborne Division and the American 82nd and 101st Airborne Divisions, in the success of the invasion.

Overall, the successful outcomes of the airborne operations during Operation Overlord were a testament to the bravery and skill of the paratroopers involved. Their actions played a crucial role in the success of the invasion and their legacy continues to be remembered as a pivotal moment in military history.

Chapter 6: The Role of Specific Military Units or Divisions in the Normandy Invasion

The 1st Infantry Division: The Big Red One

The success of Operation Overlord, the Allied invasion of Normandy during World War II, relied heavily on the strategic planning, intelligence, and espionage operations undertaken by the military. Among the various military units and divisions that played a crucial role in the invasion, the 1st Infantry Division, famously known as The Big Red One, stood out for its remarkable achievements and contributions.

The 1st Infantry Division, under the command of Major General Clarence R. Huebner, was one of the first divisions to land on the beaches of Normandy on June 6, 1944. Its soldiers faced the daunting task of securing Omaha Beach, one of the most heavily fortified and defended areas along the coast. Despite facing intense German resistance and heavy casualties, the men of The Big Red One displayed exceptional courage and determination, eventually managing to break through the enemy defenses and establish a foothold on the beach. Their bravery and sacrifice played a pivotal role in the success of the Normandy invasion.

The division's success can be attributed, in part, to the critical role played by intelligence and espionage operations. The 1st Infantry Division benefited from the invaluable information gathered by intelligence officers and spies, which helped them plan their assault and anticipate enemy movements. The division's commanders had access to detailed maps, aerial photographs, and intercepted enemy communications that allowed them to devise effective strategies and exploit weaknesses in the German defenses.

The Big Red One also showcased the important role of technology and innovation in supporting the Allied invasion. The division utilized cutting-edge equipment, such as amphibious tanks, to overcome the challenging terrain and fortified positions. The use of specialized landing craft and amphibious vehicles enabled the division to swiftly move troops and supplies, ensuring the momentum of the invasion was maintained.

Furthermore, the 1st Infantry Division faced numerous medical and logistical challenges during Operation Overlord. The division's medics worked tirelessly to provide medical aid and evacuate wounded soldiers under extremely difficult conditions. Logistical support units played a crucial role in supplying the division with ammunition, fuel, and other essential resources, ensuring the soldiers remained combat-ready.

The legacy of The Big Red One extends far beyond the success of the Normandy invasion. The division continued to play a significant role in subsequent campaigns during World War II, including the liberation of France and the Battle of the Bulge. Its soldiers exemplified the highest standards of bravery, professionalism, and sacrifice, leaving an enduring legacy in military history.

The 1st Infantry Division, The Big Red One, remains an iconic symbol of the courage and determination displayed by the Allied forces during Operation Overlord. Their contributions, along with the crucial role of intelligence, technology, and logistics, continue to be studied and celebrated by historians, ensuring that the legacy of Operation Overlord and the Normandy invasion will never be forgotten.

The 101st Airborne Division: The Screaming Eagles

One of the most renowned and revered military units of World War II, the 101st Airborne Division, known as the Screaming Eagles, played a pivotal role in the success of Operation Overlord, the 1944 Allied

Invasion of Normandy. This subchapter delves into the remarkable exploits of this elite division, examining their crucial contributions to the invasion and their enduring legacy.

The 101st Airborne Division was a key component of the overall military strategy and planning during Operation Overlord. Tasked with securing crucial objectives behind enemy lines, the division's paratroopers executed daring missions with great precision and bravery. Their primary objective was to establish and defend vital positions, such as bridges and causeways, to ensure the successful advance of Allied forces into Normandy.

Intelligence and espionage were paramount in the success of Operation Overlord, and the Screaming Eagles played a crucial role in gathering vital information. The division's intelligence officers risked their lives to obtain critical data on enemy positions, fortifications, and troop movements. Their efforts, combined with the intelligence gathered by other allied agencies, provided invaluable insights that shaped the overall strategy of the invasion.

The division's airborne operations were unparalleled in their daring and effectiveness. Dropping behind enemy lines on D-Day, the paratroopers faced formidable challenges including intense German resistance and adverse weather conditions. Despite these obstacles, the Screaming Eagles demonstrated incredible resilience and adaptability, securing their objectives and providing crucial support to the overall invasion effort.

The impact of the 101st Airborne Division on the Normandy invasion cannot be overstated. Their actions not only contributed to the success of Operation Overlord but also influenced subsequent military operations. The division's disciplined and innovative tactics, such as the use of gliders for landing heavy equipment, set a precedent for future airborne operations.

The legacy of the Screaming Eagles extends far beyond the Normandy invasion. The division went on to participate in the Battle of the Bulge and numerous other campaigns, cementing their reputation as one of the most formidable fighting forces of World War II. Today, the 101st Airborne Division remains an active and highly respected unit within the United States Army, continuing the traditions of valor and excellence established during Operation Overlord.

In conclusion, the 101st Airborne Division, the Screaming Eagles, played a critical role in the success of Operation Overlord. Their airborne operations, intelligence gathering, and unwavering determination secured vital objectives and paved the way for the Allied advance in Normandy. The legacy of this elite division endures as a testament to their bravery, skill, and unwavering commitment to the cause of freedom.

The 2nd Armored Division: Hell on Wheels

The success of Operation Overlord, the Allied invasion of Normandy during World War II, relied on the coordinated efforts of various military units and divisions. Among these, the 2nd Armored Division, known as "Hell on Wheels," played a crucial role in the invasion and subsequent liberation of France. This subchapter explores the significance of the 2nd Armored Division in the context of Operation Overlord, shedding light on its contributions, challenges, and lasting impact.

The 2nd Armored Division was a key component of the Allied ground forces during the Normandy invasion. Led by Major General Edward H. Brooks, the division boasted an impressive array of tanks, armored vehicles, and highly trained personnel. Its primary objective was to support the infantry divisions by providing armored support, breaching enemy defenses, and exploiting breakthroughs.

During the initial stages of Operation Overlord, the 2nd Armored Division faced numerous obstacles. The division encountered heavy German resistance and had to navigate through the treacherous terrain of Normandy. Despite these challenges, the division's speed, firepower, and mobility allowed it to overcome enemy defenses and secure key objectives. The 2nd Armored Division played a crucial role in the breakout from the Normandy beachhead and the subsequent pursuit of German forces across France.

The 2nd Armored Division's success can be attributed to the invaluable intelligence and espionage efforts that supported its operations. Intelligence gathering and analysis provided the division with vital information about enemy positions, fortifications, and potential weak points. This intelligence allowed the division to plan its movements and exploit enemy vulnerabilities effectively.

Moreover, the division's innovative use of technology and armored tactics significantly contributed to its success. The 2nd Armored Division utilized advanced tanks such as the M4 Sherman and employed tactics such as "blitzkrieg" to swiftly overcome enemy resistance. These technological advancements and tactical innovations revolutionized armored warfare and influenced subsequent military strategies.

The legacy of the 2nd Armored Division extends far beyond Operation Overlord. The division continued its involvement in the European theater, playing a critical role in the liberation of Paris and subsequent battles. Its success in Normandy and subsequent campaigns demonstrated the importance of armored divisions in modern warfare.

In conclusion, the 2nd Armored Division, known as "Hell on Wheels," played a vital role in Operation Overlord and the subsequent Allied liberation of France. Its armored firepower, mobility, and tactical innovations were instrumental in overcoming enemy resistance and securing critical objectives. The division's success was made possible by the intelligence and espionage efforts that supported its operations. The lasting legacy of the 2nd Armored Division can be seen in its influence on future military strategies and the recognition of the importance of armored divisions in modern warfare.

The Canadian Forces: Juno Beach and Beyond

The Canadian Forces played a crucial role in the success of Operation Overlord, the Allied invasion of Normandy during World War II. One of the most significant contributions of the Canadian military was their involvement in the assault on Juno Beach, which marked the beginning of the Canadian involvement in the invasion.

On June 6, 1944, Canadian troops stormed the heavily defended Juno Beach, facing fierce resistance from German forces. Despite the challenging circumstances, the Canadians managed to overcome the obstacles and establish a foothold on the beachhead. Their determination and courage in the face of adversity played a vital role in the overall success of the invasion.

Beyond Juno Beach, the Canadian Forces continued to make significant contributions throughout the Normandy campaign. They participated in the subsequent battles to secure the beachhead and advance further inland. The Canadian military's expertise in amphibious warfare and their ability to adapt to changing conditions were instrumental in the success of these operations.

Intelligence and espionage played a critical role in the planning and execution of Operation Overlord, and the Canadian Forces were no exception. Canadian intelligence officers provided invaluable information about German defenses, coastal fortifications, and troop movements, which helped shape the overall strategy of the invasion. The success of these intelligence efforts was a testament to the dedication and skill of the Canadian intelligence community.

The Canadian Navy also played a significant role in the Normandy invasion, providing crucial support through naval bombardment and escorting landing craft to the beaches. Their efforts ensured the safe arrival of troops and supplies, despite heavy German resistance.

Additionally, Canadian paratroopers and airborne units were deployed behind enemy lines to disrupt German communications and secure strategic objectives. Their missions were essential in disrupting enemy defenses and providing valuable intelligence to the Allied commanders.

The Canadian military's involvement in Operation Overlord was not without challenges. They faced adverse weather conditions, logistical difficulties, and medical challenges on the battlefield. However, their resilience and resourcefulness enabled them to overcome these obstacles and contribute to the ultimate success of the invasion.

The legacy of the Canadian Forces' involvement in Operation Overlord is significant. Their contributions to the liberation of Europe and the defeat of Nazi Germany are remembered and celebrated to this day. The bravery and sacrifice of Canadian soldiers at Juno Beach and beyond serve as a testament to their enduring commitment to freedom and democracy.

In conclusion, the Canadian Forces played a vital role in the success of Operation Overlord. Their involvement in the assault on Juno Beach, their contributions to intelligence and espionage efforts, and their expertise in naval and airborne operations all played a crucial role in the overall success of the invasion. The Canadian military's legacy in the Normandy campaign is one of bravery, resilience, and unwavering dedication to the cause of freedom.

Chapter 7: The Impact of Weather Conditions on Operation Overlord

The Challenges and Importance of Weather Forecasting

Weather forecasting played a crucial role in the success of Operation Overlord, the 1944 Allied Invasion of Normandy during World War II. Historians studying this pivotal event must recognize the challenges faced by meteorologists and the importance of accurate weather predictions in military strategy and planning.

Operation Overlord was a massive endeavor, involving intricate coordination of land, air, and naval forces. The success of the invasion hinged on favorable weather conditions, as the Allies needed clear skies, calm seas, and low winds to ensure a successful amphibious assault. However, the unpredictable and often harsh weather of the English Channel and the Normandy coast posed significant challenges.

Meteorologists faced the daunting task of forecasting weather patterns in the midst of war. The lack of advanced technology and limited data made accurate predictions difficult. Nevertheless, weather stations and reconnaissance aircraft were strategically positioned to gather information, while meteorologists analyzed this data to provide crucial forecasts.

The importance of weather forecasting cannot be overstated. Any delay or disruption caused by adverse weather conditions could have jeopardized the entire operation. The Allies had a limited window of opportunity due to the lunar cycle, tides, and the need for moonlight during the invasion. Therefore, accurate predictions were essential for determining the optimal date for the invasion and coordinating the various military units involved.

In addition to determining the invasion date, weather forecasts also influenced strategic decisions during Operation Overlord. For example, the decision to deploy paratroopers and conduct airborne operations depended on weather conditions, as strong winds and thick fog could scatter troops and disrupt the carefully planned assault.

Furthermore, the role of technology and innovation in supporting the Allied invasion cannot be overlooked. Advances in radar technology allowed meteorologists to track storms and monitor weather patterns more effectively. This, combined with innovative techniques such as cloud cover analysis and satellite imagery, significantly improved the accuracy of weather forecasts.

The challenges faced by meteorologists and the importance of accurate weather forecasting in Operation Overlord had a lasting impact on military operations. The success of the Normandy invasion demonstrated the critical role of intelligence and espionage, as well as the need for advanced meteorological capabilities in future military planning.

In conclusion, weather forecasting presented significant challenges during Operation Overlord, but its importance cannot be overstated. Accurate predictions were crucial in determining the invasion date, coordinating military units, and ensuring the success of the Allied forces. The role of technology and innovation in supporting weather forecasting also played a vital role in the operation's success. As historians, it is essential to recognize the challenges faced by meteorologists and their significant contributions to the planning and execution of Operation Overlord.

The Decision to Delay the Invasion

In the annals of military history, the decision to delay the invasion of Normandy on June 6, 1944, holds a significant place. Addressing historians, this subchapter delves into the intricacies of this crucial decision and its impact on Operation Overlord, the Allied invasion of Normandy during World War II. It explores the military strategy and planning that went into the delay, the role of intelligence and espionage in this decision, and the subsequent effects on naval, airborne, and specific military units involved in the invasion.

The decision to postpone D-Day was not taken lightly. It was a result of careful analysis, taking into account various factors that could potentially jeopardize the success of the operation. Intelligence and espionage played a pivotal role in providing crucial information about the German defenses, including the strength of their coastal fortifications and the presence of enemy troops in the Normandy region. This information allowed the Allied commanders to reassess their plans and modify them accordingly.

One of the primary reasons for the delay was the adverse weather conditions. The invasion required a narrow window of opportunity, when tides, moonlight, and weather would be most favorable. The decision to postpone the invasion by one day, from June 5 to June 6, was made based on weather forecasts provided by meteorologists and intelligence reports on the weather patterns in the English Channel.

The delay had significant implications on the logistical challenges faced by the Allies. It allowed for additional preparations, including the stockpiling of supplies, the deployment of more troops, and the fine-tuning of operational plans. Furthermore, it provided an opportunity for the airborne forces and paratrooper missions to be better synchronized with the naval and amphibious operations.

From a technological standpoint, the delay allowed for further innovations to support the invasion. The development of specialized landing craft, known as Higgins boats, and the deployment of Mulberry harbors, which were portable harbors used to offload supplies, were crucial advancements that contributed to the success of Operation Overlord.

The decision to delay the invasion also had important consequences for the civilian population and resistance movements in Normandy. It allowed for increased coordination with the French resistance, aiding in their efforts to disrupt German communications and sabotage enemy infrastructure.

Ultimately, the decision to delay the invasion of Normandy proved to be a critical factor in the success of Operation Overlord. It provided the Allies with a better chance of achieving their objectives and establishing a foothold in Nazi-occupied Europe. The legacy of this decision can still be seen today, as Operation Overlord remains one of the most significant military operations in history, with far-reaching consequences for World War II and the subsequent course of events.

The Weather Window for D-Day

One of the most critical factors in the success of Operation Overlord, the 1944 Allied Invasion of Normandy during World War II, was the weather. The planners knew that they needed a perfect combination of conditions to ensure the success of the largest amphibious assault in history. This subchapter will delve into the significance of the weather window for D-Day and its impact on the invasion.

Military strategy and planning during Operation Overlord heavily relied on accurate weather forecasts. The invasion was initially scheduled for June 5, 1944, but it had to be postponed due to unfavorable weather conditions. General Dwight D. Eisenhower, the Supreme Allied Commander, made the difficult decision to delay the operation by one day based on the advice of meteorologists. This delay proved to be crucial, as the weather on June 6, 1944, offered a small but essential window of opportunity.

The role of intelligence and espionage in the success of Operation Overlord cannot be overstated. Spies and informants provided vital weather information that guided the decision-making process. Meteorologists, such as Group Captain James Stagg, used this intelligence to analyze weather patterns and predict the best time for the invasion. Their expertise helped determine the specific date and hour when the weather conditions would be most favorable for the assault.

Naval operations and amphibious warfare in the Normandy invasion were greatly affected by the weather. The invasion required calm seas and low winds to ensure the safe landing of troops and equipment on the beaches. The planners also needed favorable weather conditions for air support and paratrooper missions. The airborne operations were particularly sensitive to wind speeds and cloud cover, as these factors could impact the accuracy of the drops and the cohesion of the paratrooper units.

The impact of weather conditions on Operation Overlord was not limited to the day of the invasion. Throughout the planning process, the weather was a constant concern. In the weeks leading up to D-Day, the Allies monitored the weather patterns in the English Channel and the Normandy region. They needed a break in the storms and strong winds to launch the invasion successfully.

The legacy of the weather window for D-Day extends beyond the immediate success of the operation. The meticulous planning and reliance on weather forecasts set a precedent for future military operations. The significance of meteorological intelligence and the role of technology in supporting the Allied invasion cannot be underestimated.

In conclusion, the weather window for D-Day played a pivotal role in the success of Operation Overlord. The planners had to navigate the complex relationship between military strategy, intelligence, and the ever-changing weather conditions. The careful consideration of the weather and the subsequent decision to delay the invasion by one day were essential in securing victory on June 6, 1944. The impact of the weather on the invasion highlighted the importance of accurate forecasts and the role of technology in military operations. The legacy of the weather window for D-Day continues to shape military planning and serves as a testament to the resilience and adaptability of those involved in Operation Overlord.

The Effects of Weather on the Invasion's Outcome

One of the most critical factors that influenced the outcome of Operation Overlord, the Allied invasion of Normandy during World War II, was the unpredictable and ever-changing weather conditions. Historians have long recognized the impact of weather on military operations, and the Normandy invasion was no exception.

The success of Operation Overlord heavily relied on meticulous planning, precise timing, and synchronization of multiple forces across land, sea, and air. However, despite all the intelligence and espionage efforts, one factor that remained beyond human control was the weather. The invasion was initially scheduled for June 5, 1944, but due to poor weather conditions, it had to be postponed by a day.

On the morning of June 6, 1944, commonly known as D-Day, the weather was far from ideal. Strong winds, heavy rain, and rough seas plagued the English Channel, making the amphibious assault extremely challenging. The naval operations faced significant difficulties, with landing craft struggling to navigate through the choppy waters. The rough seas also caused many soldiers to experience seasickness, further complicating the situation.

The weather also had a profound impact on the airborne operations and paratrooper missions. The dense cloud cover and low visibility hindered the accuracy of the drops, leading to widespread dispersal of paratroopers across the Normandy countryside. This caused confusion and disorganization among the troops, as they struggled to regroup and carry out their assigned objectives.

Furthermore, the weather affected aerial support and bombardment missions. Cloud cover limited the effectiveness of the air campaign, as pilots had difficulty identifying and hitting their targets. The inability to provide adequate air support put the invading forces at a disadvantage, allowing German defenses to hold out longer than anticipated.

The impact of weather conditions on Operation Overlord was not limited to the day of the invasion alone. In the days following D-Day, the Allies faced continuous challenges due to the inclement weather. Poor visibility hindered reconnaissance efforts, making it difficult to gather intelligence on enemy positions and movements. The weather also hampered the logistics of supplying troops, as rough seas and muddy terrain made transportation of men and equipment a daunting task.

In conclusion, the effects of weather on the invasion's outcome were significant and far-reaching. The inclement weather on D-Day and in the subsequent days posed tremendous challenges to the Allied forces, delaying their progress and causing operational setbacks. Despite these adversities, the Allies ultimately succeeded in establishing a foothold in Normandy, thanks to their resilience, adaptability, and the strategic use of intelligence and espionage. The weather conditions during Operation Overlord serve as a reminder of the unpredictable nature of warfare and the importance of contingency planning in military operations.

Chapter 8: The Role of Technology and Innovation in Supporting the Allied Invasion

The Development and Deployment of Mulberry Harbors

In the vast landscape of World War II, the Normandy invasion, known as Operation Overlord, stands as a pivotal moment. The success of this endeavor relied on meticulous planning and strategic execution. One of the most significant contributions to the triumph of Operation Overlord was the development and deployment of Mulberry Harbors.

Mulberry Harbors were floating artificial harbors constructed by the Allies, designed to provide critical logistical support for the invasion. These ingenious harbors were a response to the lack of suitable ports along the Normandy coastline. The German occupation had heavily fortified the existing ports, making them inaccessible for the Allied forces. Recognizing the need for a viable solution, the British engineer, Allan Beckett, conceived the idea of creating portable harbors that could be assembled and deployed quickly.

The development of Mulberry Harbors was a testament to the role of technology and innovation in supporting the Allied invasion. The harbors consisted of immense concrete caissons, known as Phoenixes, which were built in the United Kingdom and then towed across the English Channel. Once in Normandy, these Phoenixes were sunk to form breakwaters, protecting the harbor from rough sea conditions. Floating roadways, known as "Whales," connected the Phoenixes, allowing for the movement of vehicles and supplies.

The deployment of Mulberry Harbors played a crucial role in overcoming the logistical challenges faced by the Allies during the invasion. These harbors provided a secure and efficient means of unloading troops, vehicles, and supplies directly onto the beaches. This significantly expedited the process of establishing a firm foothold in Normandy, allowing for the rapid buildup of Allied forces.

Furthermore, the Mulberry Harbors showcased the role of specific military units and divisions in the success of Operation Overlord. The British Royal Engineers played a vital role in the construction and maintenance of these harbors. Their expertise in engineering and logistics ensured the smooth operation of the Mulberry Harbors, enabling the sustained flow of men and material.

The impact of weather conditions on Operation Overlord cannot be understated. The Mulberry Harbors served as a crucial buffer against the unpredictable elements. When a severe storm hit the Normandy coast in June 1944, damaging the original Omaha Beach harbor, the Mulberry Harbor at Arromanches remained intact, allowing for uninterrupted supply lines. This highlights the resilience and foresight in planning for potential weather challenges.

In conclusion, the development and deployment of Mulberry Harbors were instrumental in the success of Operation Overlord. These floating artificial harbors demonstrated the role of technology, innovation, and specific military units in overcoming logistical challenges. Moreover, they acted as a safeguard against adverse weather conditions, ensuring the sustained flow of troops and supplies. The legacy of Mulberry Harbors endures as a testament to the remarkable ingenuity and resourcefulness displayed by the Allies during the Normandy invasion.

The Use of Hobart's Funnies: Specialized Armoured Vehicles

In the lead-up to Operation Overlord, the Allied commanders faced a daunting challenge - how to successfully land troops and equipment on the heavily fortified beaches of Normandy. General Sir Percy Hobart, a brilliant British military engineer, came up with an ingenious solution:

the use of specialized armored vehicles, famously known as "Hobart's Funnies."

Hobart's Funnies were a collection of specially modified tanks and other vehicles designed to overcome the obstacles posed by the German defenses. These vehicles played a crucial role in the success of the Normandy invasion by providing the Allied forces with the necessary tools to breach the enemy's fortifications and move inland.

One of the most iconic Hobart's Funnies was the Churchill AVRE (Armoured Vehicle Royal Engineers). Equipped with a powerful 290mm petard mortar, this tank could demolish enemy strongpoints and clear a path for the infantry. Another significant vehicle was the Sherman Crab, which was fitted with a rotating flail mechanism that detonated mines, effectively clearing the way for the troops.

The ingenuity of Hobart's Funnies did not stop there. Other vehicles included the Churchill Crocodile, which had a flamethrower capable of reaching up to 120 meters, and the Churchill Ark, a floating tank that could traverse water obstacles and provide fire support to the troops.

These specialized vehicles were instrumental in overcoming the challenges posed by the German defenses. Their deployment helped the Allied forces to quickly establish a foothold on the beaches and gain a crucial advantage over the enemy. In fact, the success of the invasion can be attributed, in part, to the effective use of Hobart's Funnies.

The use of technology and innovation played a significant role in supporting the Allied invasion, and Hobart's Funnies were a prime example of this. The development and deployment of these specialized vehicles demonstrated the importance of creative problem-solving and adaptability in military operations.

Today, the legacy of Hobart's Funnies lives on. The use of specialized armored vehicles has become an integral part of modern military operations. The lessons learned from the success of these vehicles during Operation Overlord continue to influence military planning and strategy.

In conclusion, the use of Hobart's Funnies - specialized armored vehicles - played a pivotal role in the success of Operation Overlord. These vehicles provided the Allied forces with the tools they needed to overcome the formidable German defenses and establish a foothold in Normandy. The ingenuity and innovation displayed by General Sir Percy Hobart and his team continue to inspire military planners and historians alike, highlighting the crucial role of technology in supporting military operations.

The Importance of Allied Air Power

In the annals of military history, few campaigns have been as meticulously planned and executed as Operation Overlord, the Allied invasion of Normandy in 1944 during World War II. The success of this audacious undertaking can be attributed to a variety of factors, but perhaps none were as critical as the strategic deployment of Allied air power.

The role of air power in warfare had undergone a dramatic transformation during the early years of the 20th century, and by the time of Operation Overlord, it had become an indispensable component of modern military strategy. The Allies recognized the importance of air superiority in any major offensive, and thus, they meticulously planned to establish air supremacy over the beaches of Normandy.

The primary objective of Allied air power was to neutralize German defenses along the coast, disrupt enemy communications, and provide close air support to ground troops during the invasion. To achieve this, thousands of aircraft were deployed, ranging from heavy bombers to fighter planes. These aerial forces relentlessly bombed German coastal fortifications, artillery positions, and transportation infrastructure, severely hampering the enemy's ability to mount an effective defense.

Furthermore, Allied air power played a crucial role in the success of airborne operations and paratrooper missions. The use of airborne troops was a key element of the invasion strategy, as it allowed the Allies to strike deep behind enemy lines and disrupt German reinforcements. The effectiveness of these operations relied heavily on the close coordination between airborne units and the air forces, ensuring accurate drops and providing crucial air cover during their missions.

Moreover, the impact of weather conditions on Operation Overlord cannot be overstated, and once again, it was Allied air power that came to the rescue. The invasion was originally scheduled for June 5, 1944, but adverse weather forced a postponement. However, thanks to the intelligence gathered by the spies and the ability of Allied air forces to provide accurate weather forecasts, a critical window of opportunity was identified, and the invasion was launched on June 6, commonly known as D-Day.

The legacy of Allied air power in Operation Overlord is undeniable. The successful establishment of air superiority paved the way for the largest amphibious invasion in history, and the subsequent victories on the Normandy beaches marked a turning point in the war. The use of air power as an integral part of military strategy became a blueprint for future operations, and the lessons learned from Operation Overlord continue to shape modern warfare.

In conclusion, the importance of Allied air power in Operation Overlord cannot be overstated. From neutralizing enemy defenses to providing close air support, and from enabling airborne operations to accurately forecasting weather conditions, the impact of air power on the success of the invasion was immeasurable. The strategic deployment of aerial forces was a testament to the meticulous planning and coordination of the Allied forces, and it remains a shining example of the crucial role that air power plays in military campaigns.

The Contribution of Radar and Signal Intelligence

One of the lesser-known but crucial aspects of the success of Operation Overlord, the 1944 Allied Invasion of Normandy during World War II, was the invaluable contribution of radar and signal intelligence. This subchapter delves into the significance of these technologies and strategies, shedding light on their role in shaping the outcome of this historic operation.

Radar, a cutting-edge technology at the time, played a pivotal role in detecting and tracking enemy aircraft, as well as providing vital information about enemy movements and positions. By utilizing radar systems installed on ships and aircraft, the Allies gained a significant advantage in the air and at sea. This advantage was particularly evident during the naval operations and amphibious warfare in the Normandy invasion, where radar allowed the Allies to identify and neutralize German coastal defenses. Moreover, airborne operations and paratrooper missions during Operation Overlord heavily relied on radar to ensure accurate drop zones and minimize casualties. Radar technology proved to be a game-changer, enabling the Allies to achieve surprise and maintain a tactical edge over the enemy.

Signal intelligence, on the other hand, involved intercepting and deciphering coded enemy communications. This form of intelligence gathering provided the Allies with invaluable information regarding German troop movements, defensive positions, and overall military strategy. By intercepting and decrypting enemy messages, specialized units such as Bletchley Park's codebreakers were able to provide vital intelligence to the Allied commanders. This intelligence enabled the planning and execution of precise military operations, allowing the

Allies to exploit weaknesses in the German defenses and make informed strategic decisions.

The combined efforts of radar and signal intelligence greatly influenced the success of Operation Overlord. The accurate and timely information provided by these technologies allowed the Allied forces to overcome the challenges posed by the unpredictable weather conditions. By using radar, the Allies could adjust their plans accordingly and adapt to changing circumstances, mitigating the risks associated with the adverse weather.

The legacy of radar and signal intelligence in Operation Overlord is profound. Their contribution not only secured the victory in Normandy but also laid the groundwork for future military strategies and technological advancements. The role of these technologies and strategies in supporting the Allied invasion showcases their pivotal importance in intelligence and espionage during World War II. Historians studying Operation Overlord will come to appreciate the significant impact radar and signal intelligence had on the success of this monumental operation and the subsequent liberation of Europe from Nazi occupation.

Chapter 9: Medical and Logistical Challenges during Operation Overlord

Establishing Medical Facilities and Evacuation Systems

In the chaos and carnage of war, the provision of effective medical care and evacuation systems can mean the difference between life and death for soldiers on the front lines. Nowhere was this more evident than in Operation Overlord, the Allied invasion of Normandy during World War II. This subchapter explores the critical role played by medical facilities and evacuation systems in ensuring the success of the invasion.

As the largest amphibious assault in history, Operation Overlord presented unique challenges for the medical corps. The sheer scale of the operation necessitated the establishment of numerous medical facilities, from field hospitals to evacuation ships. These facilities were strategically placed to ensure that wounded soldiers could receive immediate care and be evacuated swiftly to more advanced medical facilities in England.

The planning and execution of these medical facilities and evacuation systems were integral to the overall military strategy and planning during Operation Overlord. The success of the invasion relied heavily on the ability to rapidly treat wounded soldiers and evacuate them for further care. It was essential to minimize the time between injury and treatment to increase the chances of survival and maintaining combat effectiveness.

Intelligence and espionage played a crucial role in the success of establishing medical facilities and evacuation systems. Gathering information on enemy positions, fortifications, and potential obstacles allowed Allied forces to strategically place medical facilities. Additionally, intelligence on enemy medical capabilities and evacuation routes enabled the Allies to disrupt German efforts and secure key locations for their own medical operations.

The naval and airborne operations during Operation Overlord also heavily relied on the establishment of medical facilities and evacuation systems. Naval ships were converted into floating hospitals, equipped with operating rooms and medical staff to treat wounded soldiers before they could be transported to larger facilities on land. Similarly, airborne troops had medical personnel and equipment accompanying them to provide immediate care to the wounded upon landing.

The logistical challenges faced in establishing medical facilities and evacuation systems cannot be overstated. The vast number of wounded soldiers and the need for rapid evacuation required meticulous planning and coordination. Medical supplies, equipment, and personnel had to be transported and distributed efficiently amidst the chaos of battle.

The legacy of Operation Overlord's medical facilities and evacuation systems is profound. The lessons learned from this operation shaped subsequent military strategies and planning in future conflicts. The development of more advanced medical technologies and techniques, as well as the establishment of dedicated medical evacuation units, were direct outcomes of the challenges faced during Operation Overlord.

In conclusion, the establishment of medical facilities and evacuation systems played a critical role in the success of Operation Overlord. Through effective planning, intelligence gathering, and logistical coordination, the Allies were able to provide timely and life-saving medical care to wounded soldiers, ensuring their survival and combat effectiveness. The legacy of these efforts continues to shape military medical practices to this day.

Supplying and Sustaining the Troops

In the grand scheme of Operation Overlord, the success of the Allied invasion of Normandy relied heavily on the ability to supply and sustain the troops on the ground. This subchapter delves into the intricate web of logistics, intelligence, and espionage that ensured the troops had the necessary resources to achieve victory.

Supplying the troops was no small feat. The sheer number of soldiers, vehicles, and equipment required for the invasion was staggering. The logistical challenge was further exacerbated by the need to coordinate naval operations, airborne missions, and ground forces. The success of the operation hinged on the ability to transport troops and supplies across the English Channel swiftly and efficiently. This required meticulous planning, coordination, and the innovative use of technology.

Intelligence and espionage played a crucial role in ensuring the success of the supply chain. Spies, informants, and intelligence gathering operations provided critical information about enemy positions, supply routes, and potential obstacles. This intelligence was then used to devise strategies and plans that maximized the effectiveness of supply lines while minimizing risks. The ability to intercept and decode enemy communications also provided valuable insights into their intentions and allowed for better anticipation of their moves.

Naval operations and amphibious warfare were at the forefront of the Normandy invasion. The subchapter explores the role of naval forces in transporting troops and supplies across the treacherous waters of the English Channel. It delves into the challenges faced by the sailors and the innovative tactics employed to overcome them. The crucial role of air support in providing cover for the naval operations is also examined.

The subchapter also highlights the specific contributions of airborne operations and paratrooper missions. These highly specialized units played a critical role in securing key strategic points and disrupting enemy defenses. The planning and execution of these missions required meticulous coordination with ground forces and a deep understanding of the terrain.

Moreover, the subchapter sheds light on the medical and logistical challenges faced during the invasion. The sheer number of casualties and the need to provide medical care and supplies in a fast-paced and dynamic environment stretched the resources of the Allied forces. The subchapter explores the innovative medical practices and logistical solutions that were employed to address these challenges.

The subchapter concludes by examining the long-term consequences and legacy of Operation Overlord. The success of the invasion marked a turning point in World War II and set the stage for the eventual liberation of Europe. It forever changed the face of military strategy and planning, highlighting the importance of intelligence, innovation, and the ability to sustain troops in complex operations.

For historians and enthusiasts of Operation Overlord, this subchapter provides a comprehensive overview of the vital role played by supply lines, intelligence, and logistics in the success of the Allied invasion. It explores the challenges faced, the innovative solutions devised, and the lasting impact of these achievements on military operations.

The Challenges of Casualty Management

In the grand scheme of Operation Overlord, the successful Allied invasion of Normandy during World War II, casualty management emerged as a daunting challenge. The magnitude of the operation meant that casualties were inevitable, and the ability to effectively handle and care for wounded soldiers became a critical component of the overall military strategy and planning.

The role of intelligence and espionage in the success of Operation Overlord cannot be overstated. However, even the most accurate and detailed intelligence could not eliminate the risks and dangers faced by the troops on the ground. The amphibious nature of the invasion, with naval operations playing a central role, further complicated casualty management. The landing craft, often under heavy fire from German defenses, faced significant risks, leading to casualties right from the start of the operation.

Airborne operations and paratrooper missions also contributed to the complexity of casualty management. These highly specialized units were tasked with securing key objectives and disrupting German defenses in the early stages of the invasion. However, the scattered nature of their landings and the intensity of their missions made it challenging to provide immediate medical support and evacuation for wounded paratroopers.

Specific military units and divisions played significant roles in the Normandy invasion, and their experiences shaped the challenges of casualty management. The British Royal Army Medical Corps and the American Medical Corps faced immense pressure to provide medical assistance to the wounded while dealing with limited resources and the constant threat of enemy fire.

Weather conditions also had a profound impact on casualty management during Operation Overlord. The initial plans for the invasion were delayed by bad weather, and the subsequent decision to proceed despite less than ideal conditions resulted in significant challenges. Stormy seas and low cloud cover hindered the evacuation of casualties and the delivery of vital medical supplies, exacerbating an already difficult situation.

Technological innovations played a crucial role in supporting the Allied invasion, but they also posed unique challenges for casualty management. The development of new weapons, such as the German Tiger tanks and improved artillery, led to more severe injuries that required specialized medical attention. Additionally, the introduction of new medical technologies, such as penicillin and blood transfusions, required careful coordination and logistics to ensure their effective use.

While casualty management was primarily focused on military personnel, the invasion also impacted the civilian population and resistance movements in Normandy. The presence of non-combatants further strained medical resources and created additional challenges in providing care to those in need.

In the long term, Operation Overlord left a lasting legacy on casualty management and military medicine. The lessons learned during the invasion directly influenced the development of new strategies and techniques for managing casualties in future conflicts. The experience gained in Normandy continues to shape modern military medical practices and serves as a reminder of the challenges faced by those involved in the historic invasion.

Overall, casualty management presented numerous challenges during Operation Overlord, from the initial amphibious landings to the ongoing care and evacuation of wounded soldiers. The success of the invasion hinged not only on intelligence and military strategy but also on the ability to effectively address the medical and logistical aspects of casualty management. Understanding these challenges provides crucial insights into the complexities and sacrifices associated with one of the defining moments of World War II.

Overcoming Logistical Difficulties in Normandy

The success of Operation Overlord, the Allied invasion of Normandy in 1944, hinged not only on meticulous military planning and intelligence gathering but also on overcoming numerous logistical challenges. These challenges encompassed a wide range of aspects, from transportation and supply to communication and coordination. Understanding how these difficulties were overcome sheds light on the remarkable achievements of the operation and the resilience of those involved.

One of the most significant logistical difficulties faced by the Allies was the sheer scale of the operation. The invasion required the transportation of thousands of troops, vehicles, and supplies across the English Channel. This necessitated an extensive naval operation, with numerous landing craft and warships involved. The coordination and timing of these movements were crucial to ensure that troops and supplies arrived at the designated landing zones in sync with the overall plan. Despite facing rough seas and inclement weather, the Allied forces managed to overcome these challenges through careful planning and adaptability.

Another logistical hurdle was the need to establish and maintain supply lines once the troops had landed. The successful invasion relied on a constant flow of food, ammunition, fuel, and medical supplies to sustain the advancing forces. However, the infrastructure in Normandy had been severely damaged by years of occupation and bombardment. The Allies had to quickly repair and construct harbors, roads, and railways to facilitate the transportation of supplies from the beaches to the front lines. This monumental task was achieved through the combined efforts of engineers, laborers, and military personnel, who worked tirelessly to restore the region's infrastructure under challenging conditions.

Communication posed yet another logistical difficulty. Effective communication was essential for coordinating movements, issuing orders, and relaying intelligence. However, the vast distances and rugged terrain made traditional means of communication unreliable. The Allies overcame this challenge by employing innovative technologies, such as portable radios and signal lamps, to maintain contact between units. They also utilized carrier pigeons and even enlisted the help of French resistance fighters as couriers, ensuring that vital information could be transmitted swiftly and securely.

In conclusion, the successful execution of Operation Overlord relied not only on military strategy and intelligence but also on overcoming numerous logistical difficulties. The Allies demonstrated remarkable adaptability, resilience, and ingenuity in transporting troops and supplies across the English Channel, establishing and maintaining supply lines, and ensuring effective communication. By understanding and appreciating the logistical challenges they faced and overcame, historians gain a deeper understanding of the extraordinary achievements of those involved in the Normandy invasion.

Chapter 10: Civilians and Resistance Movements in Normandy during the Invasion

The Experiences of Normandy's Civilian Population

In "The Spies Who Saved D-Day: Intelligence and Espionage in Operation Overlord," it is crucial to explore the experiences of Normandy's civilian population during the 1944 Allied Invasion of Normandy. While much of the narrative surrounding Operation Overlord focuses on military strategy and planning, the role of intelligence, and the bravery of soldiers, it is equally important to shed light on the impact of this historic event on the local population.

The Normandy invasion was an enormous undertaking that brought war directly to the doorstep of the people of Normandy. The civilian population found themselves caught in the crossfire, facing immense challenges and hardships. As the invasion approached, the people of Normandy experienced a mixture of emotions, ranging from fear and uncertainty to hope and anticipation.

The immediate impact of the invasion was the disruption of daily life. Normandy's civilians, who had been living under German occupation for several years, suddenly found themselves in the midst of a raging battle. Their homes, farms, and towns became battlegrounds, and many were forced to flee their homes to seek safety in nearby areas.

The civilian population also endured significant casualties and loss during the invasion. The heavy bombardment and fierce fighting led to the destruction of infrastructure, including homes, churches, and schools. Many innocent lives were lost, and families were torn apart.

However, amidst the chaos, the people of Normandy demonstrated incredible resilience and bravery. They provided assistance to the Allied forces, acting as guides, translators, and sources of valuable information. The local population played a crucial role in the success of the invasion, offering shelter, food, and support to the soldiers.

The resistance movements in Normandy also played a significant role in supporting the invasion. These underground networks aided in gathering intelligence, sabotaging German operations, and coordinating with Allied forces. The civilians who joined the resistance risked their lives and the lives of their families to help liberate their homeland.

The long-term consequences and legacy of Operation Overlord on the civilian population were profound. The invasion marked a turning point in the war, leading to the liberation of France and the eventual defeat of Nazi Germany. The people of Normandy, who had endured years of occupation and hardship, could finally rebuild their lives and enjoy the freedoms they had long been denied.

In conclusion, the experiences of Normandy's civilian population during the 1944 Allied Invasion of Normandy were marked by fear, resilience, and sacrifice. While they were caught in the crossfire of war, they also played a vital role in supporting the Allied forces and ultimately contributed to the success of Operation Overlord. Their stories deserve recognition and serve as a reminder of the human cost of war and the importance of remembering the sacrifices made by all those involved.

The Role of French Resistance Fighters

In the vast tapestry of events that unfolded during Operation Overlord, the pivotal role played by French Resistance fighters cannot be overstated. These courageous individuals, who operated clandestinely behind enemy lines, provided invaluable intelligence, executed covert operations, and facilitated the success of the Allied invasion of

Normandy in 1944. Their contribution not only aided in the liberation of France but also had far-reaching implications for the overall outcome of World War II.

Operating under constant threat of discovery and capture by the occupying German forces, the French Resistance served as the eyes and ears of the Allied forces. Their networks spanned across the country, gathering critical information on enemy positions, troop movements, and fortifications along the Normandy coast. This intelligence was passed on to the Allied high command, providing invaluable insights that shaped military strategy and planning for the invasion.

Moreover, Resistance fighters were instrumental in sabotaging German infrastructure and disrupting supply lines. They carried out acts of sabotage on railways, bridges, and communication networks, impeding the German war machine and hampering their ability to respond effectively to the invasion. These acts of sabotage not only weakened the enemy but also bolstered the morale of the French people, galvanizing their support for the Allied cause.

The role of the French Resistance was not limited to intelligence gathering and sabotage. They played a crucial part in facilitating the success of the amphibious and airborne operations during the invasion. Resistance fighters provided assistance to the Allied forces by marking landing zones, guiding paratroopers to their drop zones, and even engaging in direct combat against the occupying German forces.

The impact of the French Resistance on Operation Overlord extended beyond the military sphere. Their presence and activities boosted the morale of the French population, who had endured years of occupation under the Nazi regime. By actively participating in the resistance movement, civilians were able to contribute to the liberation of their country and assert their agency in the face of oppression.

The legacy of the French Resistance cannot be underestimated. Their bravery and determination paved the way for the success of Operation Overlord, and their actions continue to inspire generations. Their contribution serves as a testament to the power of ordinary individuals coming together to confront tyranny and fight for freedom. The French Resistance will forever be remembered as an integral part of the Allied victory in World War II and as a symbol of hope in the darkest of times.

Support and Collaboration with the Allied Forces

One of the key factors that contributed to the success of Operation Overlord, the Allied invasion of Normandy during World War II, was the support and collaboration between the different Allied forces. This subchapter will delve into the crucial role that cooperation played in the planning and execution of the invasion.

From the outset, it was clear that the success of Operation Overlord hinged on the combined efforts of the various Allied armies, navies, and air forces. The planning process involved extensive coordination and collaboration among the military leaders of the United States, Great Britain, and their respective allies. These leaders recognized that a unified approach was essential to overcome the challenges posed by the German defenses along the Normandy coast.

Naval operations played a pivotal role in the Normandy invasion. The sheer scale of transporting troops, equipment, and supplies across the English Channel required meticulous planning and coordination. Naval forces from various countries worked together to establish a massive fleet that would deliver the troops to the invasion beaches. The success of the naval component depended on the cooperation between different nations, as well as the innovativeness of the engineers who developed specialized landing craft and other amphibious vehicles.

Similarly, airborne operations and paratrooper missions were crucial in securing key objectives behind enemy lines. The coordination between the airborne forces and the ground troops was essential to disrupt German defenses and secure vital bridges and roadways. The success of these operations relied on accurate intelligence and effective communication between the different units involved.

Intelligence and espionage played a vital role in supporting the Allied invasion. The collaboration between the intelligence agencies of the Allied nations provided essential information regarding German defenses, troop movements, and potential landing sites. The spies and resistance movements operating in occupied France played a critical role in gathering intelligence and sabotaging German operations. The success of Operation Overlord owed much to the efforts of these brave individuals who risked their lives to aid the invasion.

The support and collaboration between the Allied forces were not limited to military operations. The invasion necessitated extensive logistical planning to ensure the steady flow of supplies, medical aid, and reinforcements. Medical personnel faced immense challenges in providing care to the wounded amidst the chaos of battle. The civilian population of Normandy also played a significant role, providing crucial support to the invading forces and participating in the resistance movement.

In conclusion, the success of Operation Overlord was a result of the extensive support and collaboration between the Allied forces. The combined efforts of the armies, navies, and air forces, as well as the intelligence agencies, spies, and resistance movements, were instrumental in overcoming the challenges posed by the German defenses. The legacy of Operation Overlord serves as a testament to the power of collaboration and unified action in achieving military objectives.

The Tragic Impact of the Invasion on Normandy's Civilians

The success of Operation Overlord, the 1944 Allied Invasion of Normandy during World War II, is often hailed as a turning point in the war. However, amidst the triumph and celebration, it is important not to forget the tragic impact the invasion had on the civilians of Normandy. In this subchapter, we will explore the untold stories of the ordinary men, women, and children who found themselves caught in the crossfire of this historic military operation.

The invasion, although meticulously planned, was an incredibly violent and chaotic event. As the Allied forces stormed the beaches, the civilians of Normandy faced the terrifying reality of war. Many were forced to flee their homes, seeking refuge in nearby towns or the countryside. Others were not so fortunate and found themselves trapped in the midst of the fighting, their lives hanging in the balance.

The devastation caused by the invasion cannot be understated. Entire villages were reduced to rubble, their once-thriving communities reduced to nothing more than ghost towns. Countless lives were lost, both through direct combat and collateral damage. The civilian death toll in Normandy was tragically high, and the psychological scars left on those who survived would last a lifetime.

In addition to the physical destruction, the invasion brought with it a wave of fear and uncertainty. The population of Normandy lived under constant threat, unsure of when or where the next attack would come. The presence of occupying forces, both Allied and Axis, further compounded their feelings of insecurity.

Yet, amidst the chaos and devastation, the civilians of Normandy displayed incredible resilience and bravery. Many joined the resistance movement, risking their lives to gather intelligence and aid the Allied cause. Their actions, often carried out in secret, played a crucial role in the success of Operation Overlord.

The tragic impact of the invasion on Normandy's civilians cannot be overlooked. Their lives were forever altered by the violence and destruction of war. It is important for historians to remember and honor their stories, shedding light on the untold sacrifices made by those who were not on the front lines.

The legacy of Operation Overlord extends far beyond the military victory it achieved. It serves as a reminder of the immense human cost of war and the resilience of ordinary people in the face of unimaginable adversity. By exploring the tragic impact of the invasion on Normandy's civilians, we gain a deeper understanding of the complexities and consequences of this historic event.

Chapter 11: Long-term Consequences and Legacy of Operation Overlord

The Liberation of Western Europe

As the subchapter titled "The Liberation of Western Europe" suggests, the content of this section will delve into the key events and strategies that led to the successful liberation of Western Europe during World War II, with a particular focus on Operation Overlord. This chapter will address historians and individuals interested in the niches of Operation Overlord, military strategy and planning, intelligence and espionage, naval and airborne operations, specific military units, weather conditions, technology and innovation, medical and logistical challenges, civilians and resistance movements, and the long-term consequences and legacy of Operation Overlord.

The liberation of Western Europe marked a turning point in the war, and Operation Overlord played a crucial role in this historic event. This section will explore the meticulous planning and coordination that went into the invasion of Normandy, examining the military strategy and planning that allowed the Allies to effectively execute this ambitious operation.

Furthermore, it will delve into the indispensable role of intelligence and espionage in the success of Operation Overlord. The section will highlight the efforts of intelligence agencies, such as the British Special Operations Executive and the American Office of Strategic Services, in gathering crucial information on German defenses and troop movements, which contributed to the Allies' ability to surprise and overpower the enemy.

Naval operations and amphibious warfare will also be extensively covered, emphasizing the challenges faced by the Allied forces in crossing the English Channel and establishing a foothold on the heavily fortified beaches of Normandy. The section will discuss the role of innovative landing craft, such as the Higgins boat, and the critical contribution of naval firepower in supporting the troops on the ground.

The airborne operations and paratrooper missions during Operation Overlord will be explored, highlighting the daring actions of the 82nd and 101st Airborne Divisions. The section will examine the glider landings and parachute drops that paved the way for the success of the amphibious assault.

Additionally, the content will address the specific military units or divisions that played pivotal roles in the Normandy invasion. It will shed light on the heroic actions of troops, such as the US Rangers at Pointe du Hoc and the British Commandos at Sword Beach, who faced fierce resistance but ultimately achieved their objectives.

The impact of weather conditions on Operation Overlord cannot be ignored. This section will discuss the challenges posed by the unpredictable weather in the English Channel, particularly the decision to delay the invasion by one day due to poor conditions and its consequences.

Moreover, the role of technology and innovation in supporting the Allied invasion will be examined. From the development of artificial harbors (Mulberry Harbors) to the use of amphibious tanks (DD tanks), technology played a crucial role in overcoming the obstacles encountered during the invasion.

The content will also shed light on the medical and logistical challenges faced by the Allies during Operation Overlord. It will discuss the provision of medical care to the wounded and the immense logistical efforts required to sustain the invasion force.

Furthermore, the section will explore the experiences of civilians and resistance movements in Normandy during the invasion. It will address the sacrifices made by local populations and their contribution to the success of the operation.

Lastly, the long-term consequences and legacy of Operation Overlord will be highlighted. This section will discuss the impact of the liberation of Western Europe on the outcome of the war and the subsequent rebuilding of Europe. It will also examine the lessons learned from Operation Overlord and its enduring significance in military history.

In conclusion, this subchapter titled "The Liberation of Western Europe" will provide historians and individuals interested in various niches of Operation Overlord with a comprehensive understanding of the key events, strategies, and factors that led to the successful liberation of Western Europe during World War II.

The Beginning of the End for Nazi Germany

In the subchapter titled "The Beginning of the End for Nazi Germany," we delve into a pivotal moment in history - the turning point that spelled doom for the Nazi regime. This period marks the culmination of Operation Overlord, the 1944 Allied Invasion of Normandy during World War II, and highlights the critical role of intelligence and espionage in its success.

As historians, we are well aware of the meticulous military strategy and planning that went into Operation Overlord. However, it is the intelligence gathered by spies that truly set the stage for victory. The Allied forces, with the help of intelligence agencies such as SOE and OSS, were able to obtain vital information about German defenses, troop movements, and strategic plans. This intelligence played a crucial role in the selection of invasion sites and the allocation of resources, ultimately leading to the success of the Normandy invasion.

Naval operations and amphibious warfare played a central role in Operation Overlord. The invasion required the coordination of an immense fleet of ships and landing craft, tasked with transporting troops, equipment, and supplies across the English Channel. The subchapter explores the challenges faced by the naval forces and the innovative solutions devised to overcome them.

Similarly, airborne operations and paratrooper missions were instrumental in securing key objectives behind enemy lines. The subchapter delves into the courageous efforts of paratroopers from the 82nd and 101st Airborne Divisions who dropped into Normandy in the early hours of D-Day, paving the way for the success of the invasion.

The impact of weather conditions on Operation Overlord cannot be understated. The subchapter examines the challenges posed by the unpredictable weather and how the Allied forces adapted their plans accordingly. It also explores the role of technology and innovation in supporting the invasion, such as the development of Mulberry harbors and the use of artificial harbors.

While Operation Overlord was primarily a military endeavor, it had far-reaching consequences for the civilian population and resistance movements in Normandy. The subchapter sheds light on the experiences of civilians during the invasion and the contributions of resistance fighters who provided valuable assistance to the Allied forces.

Finally, the subchapter concludes by exploring the long-term consequences and legacy of Operation Overlord. This momentous event marked the beginning of the end for Nazi Germany and set the stage for the eventual liberation of Europe from fascist rule. It also serves as a testament to the power of intelligence and the bravery of those involved in espionage, whose efforts proved vital in shaping the course of history.

The Birth of the United Nations

The birth of the United Nations (UN) marked a significant turning point in global history, particularly in the aftermath of World War II. As historians, it is crucial to understand the role played by the UN in the context of Operation Overlord, the 1944 Allied Invasion of Normandy during World War II. This subchapter delves into the inception of the UN, its role in shaping military strategy and planning during Operation Overlord, the significance of intelligence and espionage in the success of the operation, and its long-term consequences and legacy.

The UN was established on October 24, 1945, with the primary objective of maintaining international peace and security. However, its roots can be traced back to the early stages of World War II when the Allied powers recognized the necessity for a global organization to prevent future conflicts. The UN Charter, signed by 50 countries, sought to promote the principles of collective security, cooperation, and respect for human rights.

During Operation Overlord, the UN played a crucial role in shaping military strategy and planning. It provided a platform for the Allied powers to coordinate their efforts, share intelligence, and develop a unified approach to the invasion. The Security Council, one of the main organs of the UN, played a pivotal role in authorizing military action and resolving conflicts among the Allied powers.

Intelligence and espionage played a vital role in the success of Operation Overlord, and the UN recognized their significance in shaping military outcomes. The establishment of the United Nations Intelligence and Security Organization (UNISO) facilitated the exchange of intelligence between member states, enabling the Allies to gather crucial information about German defenses, troop movements, and strategic targets. Espionage networks, such as the Special Operations Executive (SOE), played a critical role in gathering intelligence and conducting covert operations behind enemy lines.

The birth of the UN also had a profound impact on the long-term consequences and legacy of Operation Overlord. It marked a shift towards a new world order, where collective security and international cooperation became paramount. The UN's commitment to upholding human rights and promoting peace shaped post-war reconstruction efforts and influenced subsequent military interventions.

In conclusion, the birth of the United Nations was a watershed moment in history, with far-reaching implications for Operation Overlord and its related niches. The UN provided a platform for strategic coordination, intelligence sharing, and international cooperation, all of which were integral to the success of the invasion. Moreover, the UN's legacy continues to shape global affairs, emphasizing the importance of collective security, human rights, and peaceful resolution of conflicts.